Johan

SILENCE

How to End Anxiety and Panic Forever

Johan

SILENCE

Johan

Copyright © 2023 All rights reserved. No part of this guide may be reproduced in any form without the written permission of the publisher, except for brief quotations used in articles or reviews.

Legal Disclaimer The information contained in this book and its content is not intended to replace any form of medical or professional advice, nor is it intended to substitute the need for medical, financial, legal, or other professional opinions or services that may be required. The content and information in this book are provided for educational and entertainment purposes only.

The content and information contained in this book have been collected from sources believed to be reliable and are accurate to the best of the author's knowledge, information, and beliefs. However, the author cannot guarantee their accuracy and validity and therefore cannot be held responsible for any errors and/or omissions. Additionally, the book is periodically revised as needed. If appropriate and/or necessary, it is advisable to consult with a professional (including but not limited to a medical doctor, attorney, financial advisor, or other industry professionals) before using any remedy, technique, and/or information suggested in this book.

By using the content and information in this book, you agree to hold the author harmless from any damage, cost, and expense, including legal fees, that may arise from the application of the information contained in this book. This disclaimer applies to any loss, damage, or injury caused by the application of the content in this book, directly or indirectly, under contract, tort, negligence, personal injury, criminal intent, or in any other circumstance.

You accept all risks arising from the use of the information presented in this book.

The user agrees to consult with a professional (including but not limited to a medical doctor, attorney, financial advisor, or other professionals) before using the remedies, techniques, or information suggested in this book.

SILENCE

Johan

Introduction	7
Chapter 1: My personal experiences with anxiety	10
Chapter 2: You're Not Alone!	17
Chapter 3: The positive side of anxiety	19
Chapter 4: How to explain anxiety to others	23
Chapter 5: Cognitive Thinking	26
Chapter 6: Accept or face misery	34
Chapter 7: Psychologists and Therapy	39
Chapter 8: You are "OK"!	41
Chapter 9: The secret ingredient	45
Chapter 10: How anxiety works in your body	55
Chapter 11: How anxiety works in Your Mind	60
Chapter 12: Your anxiety is fantasy!	73
Chapter 13: When there truly is something wrong	81
Chapter 14: What is a panic attack?	86
Chapter 15: The limit of your anxiety and breaking the resistance	91
Chapter 16: How your mind works	95
Chapter 17: At what point do you get stuck in the anxiety program?	105
Chapter 18: Other Root Causes (Other emotions that are blocking your feelings)	108
Chapter 19: Different Techniques (Remember your Intention and your Goal)	110
Chapter 20: Common Pitfalls	141
Chapter 21: When are your anxieties resolved?	145
Chapter 22: Medication	148
Chapter 23. Natural Alternatives to Medication	152
Chapter 24: Influence of diet on anxiety	162
Chapter 25: What's Best to Avoid?	167
Chapter 26. Bonus: the Wim Hof technique	171
Chapter 27: In Practice	175
Chapter 28: Conclusion and Closing	186

SILENCE

Johan

Introduction

There are many things that can cause anxiety and panic attacks. These things are so random that anxiety and panic can happen to anyone in the world sooner or later. For one person it comes from years of wrong upbringing. The other experiences a violent or unexpected situation. Or you are simply born with it. However, it doesn't really matter how you got your anxiety or panic attacks. Every form of anxiety, panic and depression all have one thing in common: unwanted thoughts, emotions, feelings and sensations. You'll realize after reading this book that it's not the thoughts, emotions, feelings or sensations that are the reason you experience anxiety but how you think about them.

The main reason for creating this book is because nobody told me the "secret ingredient". I've talked to many psychologists and they never explained the things you will read in this book. I noticed that many people are struggling with this. They tried so many things to get rid of their anxiety and panic attacks but nothing seems to work. Nobody told them the "secret ingredient". The thing that keeps you running in circles. I think I've found the secret ingredient. I know why you can't get rid of your anxiety and panic attacks. After reading this book, you know exactly why all the things you tried before didn't work.

I've been anxious all my life. For no apparent reason. Anxiety runs in my family. My grandmother suffered from it and my father also has anxious symptoms (he rather not talks about it..). It's therefore not surprising that this is passed on to the next generation (me). Now that I have children of my own, I also notice that my son is anxious. You can't draw conclusions from this alone but there is a clear pattern.

Because every person is different, many different types of therapies and ways to get rid of or "managing" anxiety exist.

SILENCE

While there are clearly evidence-based therapies that generally work well, they don't work for everyone. And I think the main reason is that they forget to tell you the secret ingredient. There is no step-by-step plan that everyone can follow to get rid of their anxiety. Every person is unique. With unique experiences, events and personalities. Most psychologists can't explain in detail how anxiety works. So they are trying to reduce symptoms or trying to get rid of your anxiety which simply never works.

Anxiety and panic always follow the same pattern. This is what I call the anxiety program. It's like a computer program you start up when using your computer. Whatever anxiety you suffer from, you'll always start the same program. The cause or trigger is always different, but the type of thoughts, feelings and behavior is always the same.

You're certainly not the only one with very specific anxiety and/or panic attacks. The most intelligent persons struggle with this. You're not stupid and you certainly haven't failed! The only thing you don't know yet is how anxiety and your brain works and what you're doing wrong.

I have overcome many anxieties. Social anxieties, panic attacks, anxiety about illnesses and so on. I know exactly which pitfalls there are and what your thought pattern looks like. I can very well imagine how you feel. The only difference between you and me is the subject and the experience of anxiety.

This book is divided into four themes, each with a number of chapters:

- **Theme 1:** You are not alone and totally ok!
- **Theme 2:** How does anxiety work in your body and mind?
- **Theme 3:** Various techniques on how to end the anxiety program

Johan

- **Theme 4**: Summary, useful tips and things to avoid

The best tip I can give you while reading this book is: take your time! Let the information sink in. Try things out. Stopping the anxiety program from running is not a pre-filled step-by-step plan. The different techniques you'll learn work very well for one person and not at all for another. So don't get frustrated if something doesn't work out right away. Take your time.
Various assignments:

There are several assignments in this book. These assignments vary in writing down thoughts or performing techniques in practice. My advice is to only read new chapters after you have completed the assignment. It has <u>zero effect</u> to just read the words and conceptually understand what the words mean. Take action! That also means you should not jump to the next therapy or read another book when you're done reading this one. You won't stop the anxiety program by reading books but by taking action.
Ask me a question:

Do you have a question about the book or about your anxiety? Send me an email (info@anxietyisok.com) and I will answer it as soon as possible!

Chapter 1: My personal experiences with anxiety

Important note: Some readers might trigger their anxiety if they read stories about bad things that happened to other people. There can be triggers in this chapter. If you are worried that this chapter might trigger your anxiety you can skip this chapter. Or read it when you think you're ready.

My life changed in 2014. I was 29 years old and I had a pretty normal life. I've always had mild anxiety symptoms. Especially social anxieties and hypochondria (anxiety of physical sensations in my body, anxiety of becoming sick). My social anxiety expressed itself mainly in looking up to presentations and talking to (large) groups of unknown people but also friends and family.

I've had bad skin all my life. Oily skin full of pimples. To make matters worse, my hair started falling out quite soon after puberty. Unfortunately, it runs in the family... You can imagine that I wasn't very happy about that. On a daily basis, I was inspecting my skin to get rid or hide my pimples. So other people couldn't see them. All eyes are on you during a presentation. There is a kind of pressure on your shoulders. One of my anxious thoughts was that everyone could see how bad my skin was. That wasn't the only thought, however. I also suffered from blushing (red face). During puberty, you'll soon hear this from your classmates:

"Hey, tomato!". "Can your face get even redder!?"

I can tell you that these kinds of comments don't really help you overcome anxiety... I was very nervous with every presentation or group discussion. Afraid to turn red. Afraid that people would

Johan

see my bad skin. Afraid to be the center of attention. In the end, I was afraid of what other people would think of me.

It wasn't just a red face. Sweating, tingling all over my body, feeling like running away. An extreme focus inwards. Fear of losing control. These are just the standard things I often suffered from during social situations. But It didn't control my life even though it was very annoying.

Back to 2014. I went to a festival with some friends. I was going to use ecstasy (XTC) for the first time in my life. I found it very exciting and didn't know what to expect. At a certain point, ecstasy started to do its job. I was somewhere in heaven. All my worries literally fell off my shoulders. Everything was beautiful. A feeling of extreme happiness and that for a few hours straight...

The next day nothing happened. I still felt very happy and was reminiscing about the party. But then came Monday, the Monday that changed my life. I stood up from my bed. Ready to go to work. Suddenly I became aware of dizziness. As if I had just spun three circles on a chair and then immediately stood up. I never felt this feeling in this way before. I had this dizziness all day long. I got worried pretty quickly. At that moment I was 100% convinced that the cause was ecstasy. One of my thoughts was:

> "The ecstasy has affected something in my brain that makes me dizzy forever"

An absurd thought but I believed it. I didn't even think about the fact that I had been dancing for hours in the pouring rain and cold. The fear that something had been affecting my brain was so great that I spent almost all day thinking about it. This went from bad to worse. Something you may recognize in your own anxiety is looking up information on the internet. I went online to find out how much ecstasy was appropriate for my weight. Then I found out that (obviously...) I had way too much ecstasy.

SILENCE

This, of course, reinforced the idea that the cause of my symptoms was ecstasy. That made my anxious thoughts even more intense. As a result, my focus \ attention on the dizziness became even stronger.

Five days later I was still experiencing dizziness. According to the drug information line, this couldn't be due to ecstasy use. This also reinforced my anxiety thoughts even more. instead of thinking:

> "Oh, then it must be something else"

I thought:

> "You see, ecstasy has affected my brain because it should have worn off already. I'll be dizzy forever!"

Weeks, months later, I was still dizzy. My mental focus was on the dizziness the entire day. 24/7, seven days a week. I was constantly scanning to see if I was still dizzy. Meanwhile, for the first time in my life, I had panic attacks. I was completely blown away. I never experienced panic attacks before. It's a very scary feeling. A feeling that you are losing control or that you're going to die.

Constantly paying attention and notwanting something was actually the **cause** of my dizziness. This is an important concept to understand because this is the basis of all anxiety and most depressions. **Something you don't want will grow if you give it negative attention.** The more you try to get rid of anxious or negative thoughts or feelings, the more often, harder and worse they come back. Some examples of thoughts that occur in people with anxiety and depression:

- "I want to get rid of this feeling."
- "I don't want to feel this way"
- "I don't want to think about this"
- "I want to get rid of my anxiety"

Johan

- "It will never stop…"
- Etc.

My complaints went from bad to worse. My focus went all over my body. I felt something everywhere. Eventually, I suffered from a ringing in my ears (also called tinnitus). I was focussing on the ringing in my ear all day. Afraid I would have a ringing in my ear forever. After that, I felt a feeling of stress in my stomach. Like there was a continuous release of adrenaline from my adrenal glands. That was also the thought I had. As a result, I was stressed all day because of the stress. Anxiety about anxiety.

This period lasted about a year and a half. After that, I was symptom-free within a few weeks. In fact, I even solved anxieties that had bothered me all my life. How I did this will be covered in the following chapters and themes. But although I have been symptom-free for a while, the anxiety also came back.

In 2018, disaster struck again. We (my girlfriend and I) had found out at some point that our neighbors were very angry with us about an email I sent to another neighbor several months earlier. We didn't know about this (that the neighbors were angry with us) so I wanted to solve it directly through a personal conversation. However, I noticed that I was always postponing the conversation. As a result, the tension in my body rose a little bit every day. Healthy tension is nothing to worry about. But then it happened. I suddenly became aware of the tension in my body. BOOM, all the memories from 2014 were back. The feeling of stress in my stomach. All the negative thoughts came up:

"There it is again. This is not good..."

And pretty soon I ended up back in my old thinking pattern. I literally had zero thoughts about this for many years and a

SILENCE

simple thought combined with a feeling brought everything back up. I got stuck in the anxiety program again. But I knew what it was. I had experience with it. It wasn't as bad as in 2014. Two weeks after this experience I wasn't really thinking about it anymore. Until I became pretty sick from the flu. I couldn't do anything anymore. Totally disabled, lying in bed all day long. At one point when I was downstairs to eat and drink, my girlfriend asked:

> "How's your stress and thoughts? You still have them..?"

I answered:

> "I don't really care about that anymore"

At that exact moment, I went back in my body mentally to check if the tension was still there and I felt a huge spike of tension coming up. And what happened next made everything much worse. Because I was already tired and sick, the next thought suddenly came to me:

> "I won't be able to sleep because of the tension in my stomach..."

Absurd, because I've been sleeping through the night for almost thirty years without any problems. But I believed this thought. And I completely panicked. I was convinced that I could no longer sleep because of this tension. And that actually happened. The following two weeks I slept at most three to four hours a night. During the day and in bed I had continuous panic attacks. In fact, it was so bad that I suffered from derealization. Which means it feels like you are no longer in this world. I was completely consumed by the anxiety of the tension in my stomach and not being able to sleep. That was the only thing that interested me. I could no longer drive a car, I could hardly go to the store, I could hardly do anything. I wanted to run away

Johan

from myself but I couldn't. I kept this up for two weeks and eventually, I ended up in the mental clinic.

Meanwhile, the local doctor gave me some sedatives such as oxazepam. But that didn't help at all. I received a heavy sleeping pill and antipsychotics (olanzapine) from the medical clinic. That got me back on my feet pretty quickly. But (of course) that didn't solve my anxieties. I was afraid of stress, not being able to sleep because of stress, afraid that I would no longer be able to function, afraid that I would go crazy, and afraid that I could no longer drive a car. I was actually afraid of almost literally everything...

Can you imagine this all manifested from one simple thought?

I was completely lost. I literally felt like I wanted to run away from myself. That was a very strange experience. Like you want to run out of your own head. Everything that was safe suddenly wasn't safe anymore. From that moment on my search for a solution began. I have extreme willpower and discipline. For years I've been trying to solve my anxieties. The techniques I'd used before to deal with my social anxiety weren't working. Nothing worked anymore.

The first thing I noticed was that there was no one who could immediately help me with acute anxieties. I stood with my back against the wall. Called the doctor several times. But he saw no need. "It's just anxiety," he told me. I can still get angry about it. Well, what else can you do if the doctor doesn't listen?

Most local doctors have no idea what to do with mental complaints. It might take many months or even years to get into the right program/therapy. In my case, it was so intense that they sent me to the mental clinic after two weeks of severe panic attacks. All they could do was give me heavy medication. After that, I had to wait for more than eight weeks before Icould start treatment with a psychologist. In the meantime, I tried

SILENCE

everything to get rid of my anxiety and feeling of stress. There was no one to support me. Of course, I had friends and family but they had no clue how to handle anxiety and panic attacks. And then you actually find out how few people really know how anxiety works. I was literally on my own for eight weeks. A lot can happen in eight weeks...

An advantage for me is that I'm quite open about my life. If something happens that could affect the people around me, I'll tell them immediately. Almost everyone I knew was aware of my complaints. My parents, girlfriend, friends, colleagues and my boss. Fortunately, I was not bothered by the social pressure to keep it to myself even though I had social anxieties for decades.

I know there are many people who want to keep their complaints to themselves. Because if anyone else knows, you're a weakling. Or maybe people will think negatively about you. If you have this feeling too, I can assure you that none of this is true. If you have to live with the social pressure that you can't tell anyone about your anxiety complaints, this will lead to even more complaints and social pressure.

Gradually, with the help of the techniques and especially the secret ingredient in this book, I came to realize that my anxious thoughts were fantasy. Although fantasy can certainly come close to reality. And that is what makes anxiety and panic so difficult. It all feels and looks real. But it's not. It's all fantasy made up by your own mind.

Main concepts:

- The more you try to get rid of anxious or negative thoughts, the more often, harder and worse they come back.
- Anxious thoughts can cause chronic physical complaints.
- It may take many months or even years to get in touch with a specialized psychologist.

Johan

- Few people really know how anxiety works.
- Anxiety is part of your body and mind and you can't unlearn it or forget about it. Even if you haven't had anxiety symptoms for years, they can always come back.

SILENCE

Chapter 2: You're Not Alone!

On this planet, about 264 million people suffer from anxiety and panic disorders and depressive symptoms *. In general, anxiety symptoms are more common in women. These complaints range from very mild to very serious. Sometimes resulting in death. People can't take it anymore and decide to end their lives. That has nothing to do with the anxious or depressed complaints but because of the extreme way of fighting to get rid of them. These people want to get rid of the bad feelings so badly that it consumes their entire minds and lives.

Of course, I don't know your personal situation. But It's important to realize that you're not alone. Even if you have a very specific anxiety. There's always someone on this planet who is going through the exact same thing. The problem with our society is that many people don't know what anxiety and panic is until they experience it themselves. It's therefore difficult to explain. Clueless people often give you well-intentioned advice, but that doesn't help at all. That's not surprising because when do you learn what anxiety and panic really is? Not at school, not from your parents, not from your friends…

It feels a bit like talking about kids when you don't have kids. You have an idea of what it would be like to have kids. But the real feeling only comes when your own child is born. You can't imagine that you just have to experience it. So even though you have many friends and family you can talk to about your anxiety, you may still feel alone. Even many psychologists don't even know what anxiety and panic really is. They learned it from a book but don't know what it's like to experience it in person.

Johan

Even the most intelligent people suffer from anxiety and panic. Directors of large companies, famous actors, athletes, and so on. So don't belittle yourself. There is nothing you can do about it. Simply because you never learned how anxiety works and what you are doing wrong. It's not strange at all that your anxiety symptoms don't go away or maybe even seem to get worse.

You may also have developed new anxieties in the past few years. Due to the Covid crisis and lockdowns, people no longer leave the house. Anxiety of loneliness or being locked up in your own home is quite normal. Maybe you became afraid of the coronavirus itself. Afraid that you'll get sick and die or that a family member will get sick and die. That's also very normal.

Main concepts:

- You're not the only one with specific anxiety complaints.
- Over 264 million people suffer from anxiety disorders worldwide.
- Intelligence doesn't play a role, anyone can develop anxiety and panic symptoms.

*https://apps.who.int/iris/bitstream/handle/10665/254610/WHO-MSD-MER-2017.2-eng.pdf?sequence=1

Chapter 3: The positive side of anxiety

When you read something about anxiety the word "negative" pops up many times. For almost all people it's considered a negative emotion. People want to get rid of it. We prefer to be happy all day long. But that's not realistic. Everyone in the world will feel anxiety at some point in their lives. Due to an event, a difficult situation or just plain bad luck. Try to not distinguish emotions as good or bad. As you will learn later on, positive and negative emotions <u>do not exist</u>. Replace good or bad and positive or negative with:

- Uneasy or easy
- Comfortable or uncomfortable

Turning "I feel bad" into "I feel uncomfortable".

People often forget that anxiety is precisely the reason that humanity still exists. Without anxiety, everyone would've been dead a long time ago. During our lives, we learn what to fear and what not to fear. When we learn to be afraid of something, this is called **conditioned anxiety**. For example, as a child, you sooner or later learn that a hot pan is quite dangerous and hurts. But conditioned anxiety can become a problem as soon as you become afraid of something while there isn't any real danger. For example, anxiety about social situations.

It may sound strange but anxiety has brought me quite a lot in life. I've done a lot of things (and some I still do now) because of my anxious mind. For example, I was always afraid of being late for meetings. Because I want to avoid the social confrontation (why are you late..?). So I always leave home on time. I can't remember ever being late anywhere due to my own fault. I'm also afraid of losing my phone or wallet. As a result, I always have to double-check that I have everything with me. That sounds a bit compulsive. Compulsive actions often happen from an anxious thought. For example, checking multiple times whether the door is really locked. Or that the gas stove is really off. But in my case, due to this compulsive checking, I've never lost my wallet or phone.

I also have anxious thoughts about the sports I practice. I've done many sports in my life including:

- Football;
- Kickboxing / Krav Maga;
- Bodybuilding;
- Cycling;
- Mountain biking.

I'm not talking about exercising once a week. At least three to four times a week. I often train with schedules, especially when bodybuilding and cycling. The goal is to not deviate too much from these schedules. Otherwise, you might as well quit if you miss a workout every week. At least, that's how I think about it.

I was and am mainly result-oriented. If I missed a training I was afraid that I would fall behind and that my training schedule would no longer be correct. Or that I would be less strong than my friends who were also training hard. Behind every workout was anxiety about missing progress. This anxiety resulted in a very strong discipline in everything I do. I never skipped a workout. Of course, there were times when I didn't feel like training at all. But I still exercised. In the end, I was always happy that I did the training. If I wasn't afraid of missing progress I would've given up much earlier and would probably not have achieved my many sporting goals.

A funny example of my determination is the first time I went to the gym. I was about 25 years old and started pumping iron with

SILENCE

some colleges. After just two months, I was the only one still going to the gym... It was very simple for me:

> "I paid for a full year subscription so you're going to stick with it!"

But I also learned, by chance, that my anxiety is fantasy. I went on holiday to Portugal. I was looking forward to that, but I wouldn't be able to work out for a whole week! There goes my progress! At least, that's what I thought. The opposite happened. Because I stopped training for aweek, my muscles had time to adapt. They started to grow! As I lay on the beach with a cocktail in hand. That was the realization for me that it's not bad at all if you don't train for a week.

My anxiety/belief was:

- "I can't train for a week, I'm losing muscle mass and progress!"

The reality was:

- "My muscles started to grow because I finally gave them a rest"

So my anxiety was a fantasy I had made up myself. The disaster scenario that I would miss progression did not come true at all. In fact, the opposite happened!

Another example of how anxiety helps me is healthy eating. I simply can't eat too bad because if I do I'm afraid it's not healthy for my body. That's why I can eat a container of green food every day effortlessly. I don't buy large bags of chips but at most 150 grams. I'm always the only one to scrape black pieces off my burned meat when it's a little too well done... A bit compulsive, but because of that I generally eat very healthy and eat relatively little amounts of junk foods.

Johan

For me personally, it's literally impossible to become overweight. That's not because of genetics but simply thoughts. Because adding weight triggers my anxiety that it's not healthy to become overweight so I eat more healthy things and exercise more.

Writing this book also stems from my discipline and perseverance. In addition to my forty-hour work week, I'm often busy with other projects, including writing this book. Despite having a family with two children. Many people think I'm crazy. But if you don't take action, nothing will change. Just as much that everything you have achieved in your life so far is a result of the actions you have taken. Based on the thoughts you had! Nothing will change unless you take action.

Don't view your anxiety as just a negative emotion. In fact, without the emotion of fear, you would no longer be alive!

Assignment: Think about your current anxieties and write down the positive things it has brought you. Is your anxiety really just a negative emotion that you want to get rid of?

Main concepts:

- Anxiety is not a negative emotion;
- Anxiety can also bring you positive things;
- Without anxiety, everyone would've been dead long ago;
- The anxious thoughts you have might be fantasy;
- Replace the word "negative" with "uncomfortable" or "uneasy".

Chapter 4: How to explain anxiety to others

How would you explain to someone else what you feel when you experience anxiety and panic attacks?

For me personally, it was a continuous focus on bodily sensations. With all kinds of thoughts about not wanting to feel these sensations. Feeling like losing control. People understood it a bit but couldn't imagine how that feels in detail. My girlfriend also suffered from anxiety and was often concerned with this when we watched a movie. She indicated that she was unable to follow the movie properly due to her anxiety. I didn't understand any of this. I always said: "Just go watch the movie…". I didn't know any better. How can you not concentrate on watching a movie, I thought. Until I had to deal with anxiety myself… Now I know exactly what my girlfriend meant.

Few people know how anxiety really works. So you quickly get well-intentioned advice such as:

- "It's all in your head.."
- "Don't worry so much…"
- "Just go do something else."
- "Focus on something else.."
- "Take a vacation".
- Etc.

You probably heard them all. But you can't blame them either. Although tips are well-intentioned, they're often useless. Let me explain why.

There is another emotion that, like anxiety, can rule your life:

Johan

- You forget things;
- You're going to do things you wouldn't otherwise do;
- You spend all day thinking about it and can't get it out of your head;
- You lose your concentration and you try to distract yourself, but it doesn't work.

These are all things you often see in anxious people. Continuous thoughts about a certain subject that you can't get out of your head. But this is not about anxiety but another emotion. Do you already have an idea?

Falling in love! Anxiety and love are very close to each other when you look at the behavior and thought patterns. What do you do when you're in love with someone? You spend all day thinking about that person and can't get him or her out of your head. You've probably heard the saying "Love makes you blind". People who are madly in love don't have a clear view of reality. Because you are so in love, other signals go unnoticed or are simply ignored.

And sometimes being in love is a big deal. Because if you're in love but the person in question is not in love with you, what will you do? Did your crush just disappear? Are you going to continue as if nothing happened? Sometimes you just can't get someone out of your head. Would it help if someone said to you:

- "It's between your ears.."
- "Don't worry so much…"
- "Just go do something else."

Are you suddenly not in love anymore? No, of course not. Anxiety works in exactly the same way. Anxiety blinds. You no longer see reality and start doing things you would never do otherwise. Like avoiding places or situations. Because you pay too much attention to certain feelings, you no longer feel other

SILENCE

"positive" feelings. If you explain your anxiety to someone else as falling in love with someone, they probably can empathize much better. Because everyone has been falling in love sooner or later in their lives. Some people need years to let go of their childhood love. Anxiety and love can become an obsession with dire consequences. But a life without both is also unimaginable. Even if you wish anxiety didn't exist right now.

Main concepts:

- The emotions anxiety/fear and love are very similar;
- Well-intentioned "tips" are of little use in dealing with anxiety and panic.

Chapter 5: Cognitive Thinking

We are the only species in the world that has the ability to think cognitively. This means you can **think about what you think and feel**. Other animal species are unable or hardly able to do this and act on instinct. Being able to think cognitively has brought us everything we have in the world today. Insane inventions, smartphones, computers, airplanes, the internet and so on. On the other hand, we also have poverty, wars, anxieties and panic attacks.

The only reason you have anxiety, panic attacks and even depression is because you **think about** what you think and feel **in a negative way**.

You can't suffer from any anxiety, panic or depression when you don't think about it!

But you can't give your mind the command to stop thinking about something. Because your mind does not have the ability to stop thoughts. Your mind only has the ability to add up or multiply thoughts. You can never make thoughts go away or forget them. More about this later on.

SILENCE

How does cognitive thinking work:

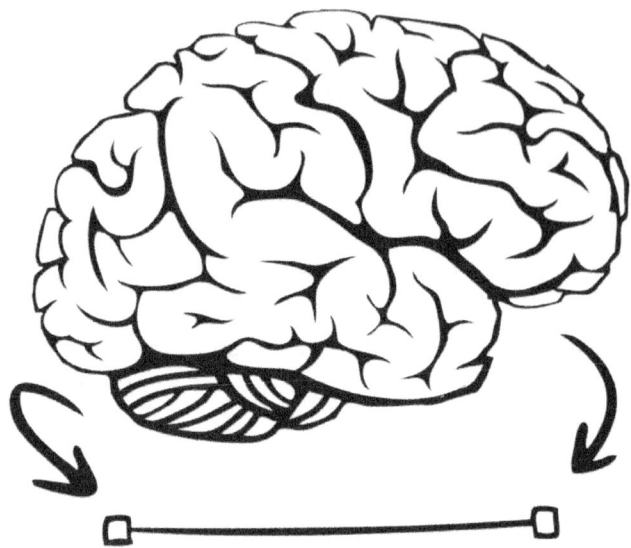

This line is a reflection of your mind. You can place all kinds of thoughts between the two endpoints. But there is a limit to how many thoughts you can have. For example, you can't think about ten things at once. You can't be at work, meanwhile making a shopping list and working out your finances. You can think about one or two things with great attention at the most, but after that, you'll lose focus.

What thoughts come to your mind have to do with:

- How you were raised;
- How you grew up in general;
- What you've been through (your experiences);
- Genetically determined;
- Your beliefs;

- Etc.

Everything you **identify** within life will cause thoughts to be produced in your subconscious mind. To identify means to appropriate, to agree with, to support, to believe. It doesn't matter if it's really true what you've been identified with. As long as you are convinced it is true, this will express itself in your subconscious mind.

Right now you are completely identified with your anxiety. The trick is to separate this identification from who you really are. You are not your thoughts, you are the one **observing your thoughts**. Even if you have no thoughts at all, you are still present and alert without doing anything. As soon as you realize that your thoughts are just thoughts and you can observe them instead of identifying them (going along with your thoughts) your anxiety and depression will melt like snow in the sun. More on this in later chapters.

Someone who is cycling around and lives without anxieties or other worries has the following thoughts in random order:

- "What a lovely weather"
- "What a beautiful environment"
- "I will cycle past here more often"
- "Maybe I will stop by there and there"
- "Hey, I feel my heart skip a beat…"
- "Oh yes, I have to get some groceries later so I need to head home soon"
- "Hey, there's Larry…."

His\her entire mind is filled with neutral thoughts of the moment. Without anxieties and without worries about the past or future. But someone who is anxious about physical sensations might have the following thoughts:

- "What a lovely weather"

SILENCE

- "Maybe I will stop by there and there"
- "Ohh no, did I feel my heart skip a beat there again?"
- "This doesn't feel right.."
- "I should call the doctor when I get home.. This is already the third time this week"
- "I'm going back home, I don't trust this…"
- "What if I have a heart attack in the middle of nowhere!?..."

Both persons experience the exact same sensations. Only person B starts to worry about his own thoughts and feelings and starts the anxiety program. The more you worry, the more weight you give to certain thoughts and feelings. **It's not the feeling that makes you anxious, but the thoughts you have about the feeling.** This is important to remember because this is the basis of any anxiety. Anxiety isn't about what you feel or have experienced, but how you think about these experiences.

People with extreme anxieties have their entire mind flooded with negative thoughts. In the meantime, these individuals fully identify with these thoughts. They totally believe these thoughts are true:

- I am depressed;
- I am good-for-nothing;
- I can't do anything;
- I can't leave my house anymore;
- What will other people think of me?;
- I can't handle this;
- Why do I feel this way…;
- Etc.

This causes your mind to be engulfed by negative thoughts. If you are going to visualize this, it could look like this:

Johan

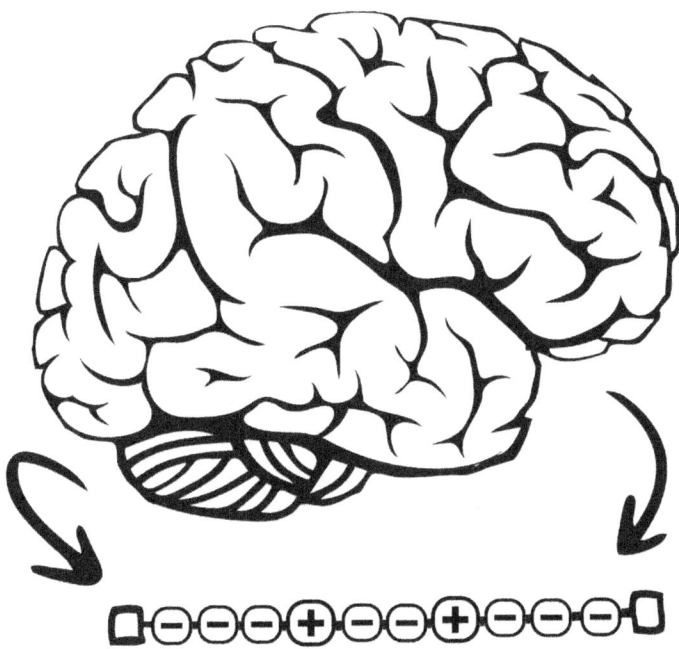

All the + are positive or neutral thoughts and all the - are negative thoughts. The more negative you think, the less room is left for positive thoughts. So it makes sense that people who are depressed don't see the positive things anymore. There is simply no more room for positive thoughts.

Even though you're doing things that you enjoy, you can still be completely consumed by negative thoughts. This ensures that you can no longer be fully in the present moment. Because you're always preoccupied with negative thoughts or feelings. If we take another look at the thoughts of above example:

- "What a lovely weather"
- "What a beautiful setting here"
- "I will cycle past here more often"
- "Maybe I will stop by there and there"
- "Hey, I feel my heart skip a beat…"

SILENCE

- "Oh yes, I have to get some groceries later so I don't have to cycle too far"
- "Hey, do I see a well-known person there.."

This person's mind is completely filled with positive or neutral thoughts:

A "negative" feeling passes by (the minus) but this person doesn't respond to it. This person doesn't care if his/her heart skips a beat. Person B suffers from hypochondria and thinks there is something wrong with his heart:

Then all sorts of catastrophic thoughts come up. And that's exactly the point when things go wrong. This person can do two things. Don't respond to catastrophic thoughts or identify with them. You can't prevent thoughts about a specific subject from popping up into your mind as long as you're afraid of something. But you can decide whether to identify with it or not. The stream of thoughts could also look like this:

- "What a lovely weather"
- "Maybe I will stop by there and there"
- "Ohh no, did I feel my heart skip a beat there now?"
- "Keep calm, nothing is wrong"

Johan

- "My heart skips a beat, that can happen. That happens to everyone"
- "Thank you amygdala (part of the brain that regulates anxiety) for warning me, but my heart is already checked by the doctor and nothing is wrong."
- "I am now going to enjoy the area again"
- "Ohhh, I have to go to the store soon…"

The stream of thoughts then looks like this:

By thinking differently, you can exclude other negative thoughts. In this case, the heart of person B was looked at by a heart specialist. There is nothing wrong with this person's heart at all. Getting checked by a specialist can be a great reassurance that reduces anxiety. But for another person it's not reassuring at all:

> "My heart is still skipping a beat, **what if** the doctor missed something…?"

Now you end up in a stream of thoughts from which it's very difficult to get out. There is no doctor who can tell you with 100% certainty that there's really nothing wrong. It's therefore important that you can deal with uncertainty and recognize that you simply can't know everything.

Anxiety can arise from different emotions, sensations, thoughts and feelings. These emotions, sensations, thoughts and feelings are always <u>neutral</u>. **We make them positive or negative by thinking about them**. Without thinking, anxiety, panic attacks and depression can't exist.

SILENCE

Assignment: When do anxious and or negative thoughts take you over? Is that during a certain situation? Or as soon as you get out of bed? Write down a few scenarios where your anxiety program seems to take over. What thought does it start with? When do you start identifying with your anxious thoughts?

It's important to remember these thought patterns. At some point, you learn to recognize them. You become aware of how you think. It may surprise you, but 99% of people are not aware of what they're thinking. They are completely absorbed in their thoughts and do not recognize their own thinking patterns. When it comes to anxiety, it's important to be <u>conscious</u> at the moment when anxious thoughts enter your mind. Once you can recognize these thoughts, you can change them or respond in a different way instead of your automatic response.

Write down a situation when you were not bothered by your anxiety. What thoughts did you have regarding your anxiety?

We will use the answers from this assignment in later chapters.

Main concepts:

- Cognitive thinking means thinking about what you are thinking or feeling;
- It is not the situation or feeling that makes you anxious, but how you think about the situation, feeling, sensation, thought, emotion, etc;
- Emotions, sensations, thoughts and feelings are always <u>neutral</u>. **We make them positive or negative by thinking about them;**
- 100% certainty doesn't exist;
- Your mind can handle a maximum number of thoughts. If your mind is completely full of negative thoughts, there is no room left for positive thoughts.

Chapter 6: Accept or face misery

I get asked many times how to accept anxiety. But that's a trap many people fall into. Because this question implies that you <u>need to do something</u> to accept anxiety. Many people get caught up in trying to accept their anxiety. They think that accepting is something you need to do. Accepting actually means that you <u>stop doing something</u> (stop trying to get rid of it). You can't consciously accept something. Because when you are consciously thinking about it you don't accept it.

What are you doing when you 100% accept something? Nothing! You simply don't think about it in any way. Accepting your anxiety means that you are less involved overtime. That your urge to change or get rid of it is gradually stopping. When you accept your anxiety 100%, you are simply not thinking about it. You are not trying to change it.

So it's good to realize that you can't accept something by thinking about it! In reality, when you experience something new or get new insights your thinking changes. For example, using one of the exercises in this book might help you reduce your anxiety. You experienced something new and that will make your (future) thoughts change.

But you can't think:

"How am I going to accept this..."

without having any new insights or experience and then expect you are going to find a way to accept your anxiety.

Accepting is not something you can do. There is no "how". You need to <u>stop</u> doing something. Whenever you read something

SILENCE

about "accepting" or "acceptance" in this book, that means that you need to stop doing something.

Whenever you get thoughts about "how to accept your anxiety" then be aware of these thoughts. And realize that these exact thoughts prevent you from accepting your anxiety. You are still looking for a way to get rid of it or change it.

When anxious thoughts or feelings come to mind, you can cognitively do several things:

- Ignore them;
- Push them away;
- Fight against them.

Or

- Greet them;
- Challenge them;
- Let them be (don't engage).

There is a fine line between these options. Ignoring thoughts and feelings can work well in the short term. However, there's a good chance that they'll come back later. If you start suppressing thoughts and feelings, they'll come back pretty quickly. Because there is a reason why you push them away (you don't want to think about or feel them).

People who experience anxiety and panic are very busy ignoring and suppressing emotions, sensations, thoughts or feelings. The more intense and more often you experience anxiety, the harder you are fighting against thoughts and feelings you want to avoid.

If you want to control something you can't control, the only possible outcome is misery. Anxiety and control often go hand in hand. To visualize:

Johan

```
   ☺         ☹         😭
━━━━━━━━━━━━━┳━━━━━━━━━━━
Acceptance   ┃           Misery
            ⇨
     It needs to go!
       (resistance)
```

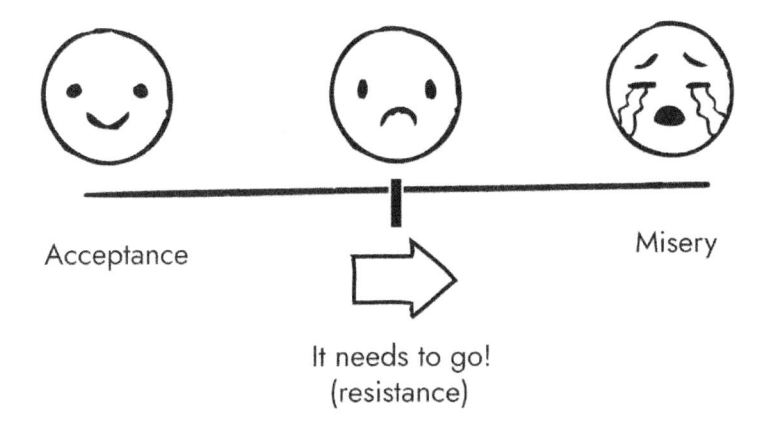

Some people only experience anxiety in certain situations. Other people are anxious all day. These people are miserable 24/7. They are no longer themselves. Anxious thoughts are always present. And if you're not careful, that misery can turn into complete misery. Think of a (severe) depression. People who don't want to feel anxious are constantly looking for a solution and resisting negative thoughts and feelings:

- Why do I feel this way?
- When will it end!?
- It must go!
- I can't do this anymore…
- Stop!
- What if…

What these people often don't realize is that they're working further and further towards misery. What's the opposite of resistance?

SILENCE

Acceptance ← Bring it on! → *Misery*

The only way to deal with your anxieties is to face them, greet them or let them be. That's of course a big cliché. But challenging them, investigating them and most importantly, greeting them will slowly decrease your resistance against them. And with that, your negative thoughts and feelings automatically decrease. Up to the point they don't even come up in your subconscious mind anymore.

Now the goal isn't to fully accept everything that happens to you. Even the most relaxed people in the world (think of monks in Tibet) can't even do that. So don't put pressure on yourself. By the way, you can apply the above to many things. Even the simplest things can make you feel miserable. Think of a moment when you drive home from work and end up in a traffic jam in which you get stuck for at least an hour. What are you going to do?

Are you going to accept that you're stuck in a traffic jam and have to wait at least another hour? Or are you going to swear at all those people who are also stuck in traffic, changing lanes all the time to get out of that traffic jam as quickly as possible?

The only thing that happens when you don't accept the current situation is feeling miserable. Unless you have control over the situation. For example, you may feel very miserable because you're overweight. But you can do something about that. You can feel very miserable because you're anxious every day. But you can do something about that. You can't do much about a traffic jam.

When you look at it this way, you can sort of pick your "battles". Fighting over things you can't control will only make you miserable. You'll therefore never "win" these battles. Almost all people who have anxiety or panic attacks try to control and overcome their feelings, thoughts, and emotions. However, you can't control emotions and you certainly can't win from them. The only thing you can do with emotions is **let them be**.

You won't learn anything in this book that will make your anxiety go away. You'll also learn nothing about how to win or overcome your anxiety. That's not possible. You are going to learn how to be "OK" with your thoughts, feelings, emotions and sensations.

Main concepts:

- People who don't want to feel anxious are constantly looking for a solution against negative thoughts and feelings.
- If you try to control situations that can't be controlled, it always results in misery.
- Choose your battles. You don't always have to fight your thoughts or feelings.
- The only thing you can do with emotions, thoughts and feelings is **let them be**.

Chapter 7: Psychologists and Therapy

You may have had many conversations with one or more psychologists. Or maybe you're afraid to talk to a psychologist. Or you prefer to try to solve it yourself first. Whatever the reason for talking to a psychologist or not, do what makes you feel comfortable.

The problem with psychologists is that they can never fully empathize with what you're going through. This is only possible if the psychologist also endured anxieties or panic attacks. That's often not the case and that can immediately create a bit of a distance. A psychologist then acts from theory. Admittedly based on a theory that has been scientifically proven to be effective.

Also, a psychiatrist might introduce you to medication sooner or later. It's therefore important to be well prepared when starting treatment. For example, what are the consequences of taking or not taking medication? Medication is often referred to too quickly. Medication is really the last step in treatment. It doesn't help solve the problem, has unpleasant side effects and anxiety can return once you stop. A much better alternative are natural herbs that have been scientifically proven to work just as well as antidepressants but without side effects. You can read more about this in theme four.

What you need is someone:

- Who can explain in detail how anxiety works;
- Can explain in detail what you are doing wrong;
- Who has experienced anxiety and panic themself;

Someone who knows exactly how you feel and how you think. Not just from theory. Going to therapy doesn't always have the desired effect. That doesn't mean that psychologists who haven't experienced anxiety or panic can't help you.

If you're currently undergoing treatment, it's not wise to mix things up. Always focus on one treatment at a time. If you want to use this book as an aid in your treatment, make sure that your practitioner is aware. Not all psychologists know how to solve anxiety and panic attacks. That may sound weird but on the other hand, it makes sense. Because how can you solve a problem for someone else if you've never experienced it yourself? It is like telling someone how to raise kids while you don't have kids. Or telling someone how to lose weight while you never experienced being overweight.

What also doesn't help is that psychologists are not **_allowed_** to deviate from a particular theory. It's required by law that they adhere to a certain trajectory. Alternative techniques and exercises will therefore not be discussed. For the simple reason that a professional practitioner is legally responsible for the treatment and the consequences.

Don't get me wrong, there are plenty of psychologists who can help you. But do you know in advance who will treat you and whether this person can help you? It makes quite a difference if a starting psychologist with barely any experience helps you or someone who has been in the profession for thirty years and has overcome anxiety and panic themself.

Main concepts:

- Many psychologists have not experienced anxiety or panic themselves and act from theory;
- Medication is prescribed far too often and too quickly;
- Try to find a psychologist (if you need one) who also experienced anxiety and panic.

Chapter 8: You are "OK"!

People who have been treated by a psychologist always receive a label. For example, you have a:

- Anxiety disorder;
- Panic disorder;
- Compulsive disorder;
- Social anxiety disorder;
- Compulsive anxiety disorder;
- Personality disorder;
- Etc.

Some people are sensitive to that. Oh dear, I have a disorder! But the word "disorder" suggests that something is wrong with you. That certain connections in your head are not functioning correctly. That something is wrong with your brain. That you have some kind of illness. Anxiety, panic and depression are not diseases. It's a result of a wrong thinking pattern. Or rather the resistance to negative thoughts and feelings. Which you have complete control over. Even if it doesn't feel that way. Of course there are exceptions where there is a medical cause such as bipolar disorder or autism but in most cases there is no real medical cause. <u>Anyone</u> can develop anxiety or depression sooner or later in life. But it's also true that some people are more susceptible to developing anxiety and depression than others.

Millions of people who suffer from anxiety or panic take medication. Usually you take medication because you are sick or something needs to be cured. Most medication is just symptom relief. If you have a headache you take an aspirin and a nasal spray if you have a bad cold. However, with anxiety or panic there is nothing wrong with your body or your brain. There is nothing broken, you are not sick, you have a wrong thinking pattern.

Johan

With anxiety and panic it's often suggested that neurotransmitters in the brain don't have the right balance. Antidepressants act on these neurotransmitters and can therefore reduce anxiety and panic. But that would also mean that people who are completely healthy with a healthy hormonal balance can never develop anxiety or panic symptoms (which is not true at all). Or that people who suffer from anxiety and panic can never solve this without medication because there is always an imbalance in the brain (which is not true at all).

It's <u>never</u> been scientifically proven that someone with anxiety and panic is dealing with an imbalance of neurotransmitters in the brain. That is a myth and only a hypothesis. The brain is far too complex and consists of thousands of different substances. I've had social anxiety for 25+ years. I've learned to think differently and now my social anxiety program has stopped running. That had nothing to do with substances in my brain. I learned how anxiety works and how to rewire my thought patterns.

I've also helped many people with anxiety and other mental problems like burn-out or depression. Most experience immediate relief after finding out what they are doing wrong all these years. They learned to look at their thoughts in a different way and rewired their brain. And you can learn this too!

That's not to say that there are no medical causes at all. You often see in people with depression that there is always someone in the family who also suffers from it. So many things affect how you think and who you are as a person that a pill is not going to fix that. Antidepressants are mainly symptom relief. It may very well help but will never solve the underlying problem. In addition, there are millions of people who take antidepressants but still suffer from anxiety or panic. If you stop taking medication and don't have the right treatment, there is a high chance that the anxiety will return.

SILENCE

You're totally fine! You have a disturbed thinking pattern. This can be solved without medication. Sometimes it's so intense that it's not possible without medication. And that's totally okay too! As a matter of fact I needed some severe medication (olanzapine) to get back on earth. But my intention was always to get rid of medication as soon as possible. Just be aware of what you are doing. And what resources you use. Medication should only be taken if there really is no other option and you have done everything you can.

It's no discussion that antidepressants don't work or are of no use. Only it doesn't solve the underlying problem. Just as well that after drinking alcohol or taking drugs you always become "you" again when the alcohol and drugs wear out. You can't solve mental problems by simply releasing some extra happiness hormones or numbing your brain. That's why I believe that it's very dangerous to just prescribe medication for anxiety and panic. Antidepressants are not the same as taking aspirins.

On the other hand, you can also see medication as swimming armbands. When you learn to swim, you first need armbands. Antidepressants can be the armbands that help you with treatment. Sometimes the anxiety and panic is just too intense and you need medication. This is totally ok! Just be aware of psychologists who want to put you on medication for no obvious reason.

There's also another option: alternative medication in the form of various herbs. These herbs are scientifically proven effective, completely safe and can have the same effect as antidepressants. Personally, I benefited a lot from this. You can read how antidepressants work and which natural alternatives there are in theme four. Do note you should never ever use these herbs if you are on medication.

Johan

Main concepts:

- **You're totally fine!**
- You don't have an imbalance of neurotransmitters. This has never been proven;
- Everyone in the world can experience anxiety, panic and depression;
- You're not sick, you got stuck in a wrong thinking pattern.

Chapter 9: The secret ingredient

This is the most important chapter in this entire book. You're going to learn why you get stuck in anxious thoughts and what you are doing wrong in your thinking pattern. In the introduction of this book I named the process of anxiety and panic the "anxiety program". See your mind as one big computer. Every electronic device on this planet needs an operating system and other programs to function. A smartphone without an operating system (Android, IOS) is useless. And your computer or laptop needs Windows, Mac OS or Linux before you can use them.

Our mind also has a few operating systems. These are preinstalled programs we call emotions. If you want, you can change the operating system and programs on your computer, laptop or phone. You can decide to install/update to a new version or remove it. You can also choose to stop using a certain program.

The main difference is, you <u>can't change</u> the operating system in your mind. You can't:

- Remove programs
- Consciously stop them from running
- Change programs

For example, when you see something funny you need to laugh. It's not possible to prevent the humor program from starting. However, this program is not always started for everyone in the same situation. Something that makes you laugh does not mean everybody will laugh about it. But the fundamental working of the humor program is exactly the same for everyone. The only difference is the trigger. With trigger I mean the situation that makes you laugh.

When you try to stop the humor program from running, bad things happen. Imagine you're sitting in a silent coupe in the train full of people. You see something extremely funny on your phone. What will happen? You try holding back your laugh. Because it's socially inappropriate to laugh out loud in a silent coupe. While doing so, you:

- Get a red face
- Start to splurge
- You put your hands in front of your mouth
- Etc.

You'll try anything to hold back your laugh. What you are really trying to do is stop the humor program from running. In reality, nothing bad happens when you try to stop the humor program from running beside the things listed above. Eventually, the humor program will stop running automatically (at some point it's not funny anymore). After that you go on with your day like nothing happened.

Every emotion works fundamentally in the same way. The difference is, most people don't want to start the anxiety program. And when it does start, they try to stop it. Because the anxiety program isn't that funny... But just like the humor program, the anxiety program will stop running automatically. You don't have to do anything to make it stop. But this is exactly the point where things go wrong. People are <u>desperately</u> trying to stop the anxiety program from running. Because they don't want the accompanying thoughts and feelings the anxiety program produces. So they try:

- Changing the program (for example, forcing positive thoughts)
- To stop the program from running (trying to get rid of it)

SILENCE

- Basically they never want to start the anxiety program <u>ever again</u>.

But just like the humor program, trying to stop the anxiety program from running has consequences:

- Anxiety complaints
- Endless loops of negative thoughts
- Feelings of stress

The more you try to stop the anxiety program from running the worse the consequences:

- Panic attacks
- Burn-out
- Depression
- Desperation and hopelessness (I will never get rid of it!)

You can't change the programs (emotions) in your brain. Ofcourse, you can learn or experience new things. And these experiences can change the trigger that causes the program to run. For example, as a child you were laughing at Bugs Bunny and now you might be a fan of "The Office". The humor program still runs and functions in the exact same way. Only the trigger changed. You can also experience that the things you fear are not that scary. And that prevents the anxiety program from running the next time.

When is something not funny anymore? When you have seen it too many times. You already know what will happen. When is anxiety not that scary anymore? When you let it happen too many times. You already know what will happen (nothing!). But people with anxiety won't let it happen. They think something really bad is going to happen when they let the anxiety program run.

Johan

What is the root cause of your current anxiety, panic or whatever mental complaint you have:

You are trying to stop the anxiety program from running!

With thoughts like:

> "My anxiety needs to go…"

Or

> "I don't want to feel X anymore"

Anxiety will never go away. That's impossible because anxiety is an emotion. It's a preinstalled program you can't remove. Whatever your problem is right now, it can never be the goal to:

- Make it go away or stop
- Not wanting it anymore or change it
- Not wanting to think about it

Actually, it's the exact opposite:

> "**STOP** trying to get rid of your anxiety!"

The main goal of this book is to let you realize that being "OK" with your thoughts, sensations and feelings means <u>you need to stop trying to get rid of your anxiety complaints</u>. Stop trying to solve the problem. It's not your sensations, feelings or thoughts that are the problem but your urge to solve this "problem". Your urge to stop the anxiety program from running. But there is no solution for this problem. The only solution is to let the anxiety program run. It will stop running automatically. You don't have to do anything to stop it. This is exactly the reason why you still haven't found a solution. You are **continuously doing something** trying to stop the anxiety program from running.

SILENCE

You can't remove emotions or make them disappear. Let's say from today you decide not to laugh again for the rest of your life. Because you disabled your happy emotions. Isn't it absurd to never laugh again your entire life? What happens when you need to laugh but try to hold it back? No matter how hard you try, it will come out eventually.

Anxiety works in the same way. But what are you doing right now with anxious thoughts and feelings? You try to stop it, thinking it away or cursing it. With all its consequences.

There is no magic exercise or technique that will make you accept your anxiety. Or a way to "deal with it". Is this recognizable? That you're continuously looking for a way to change your feelings to make them less annoying or make them go away? Doing things like breathing exercises or meditation. Did that help?

It might look like that your brain is working against you or that something is wrong. But there is nothing wrong. You are continuously giving your brain the instruction to stop the anxiety program from running. But your brain does not understand this instruction! You are actually giving your brain the instruction that this (what you fear) is important to you. So what will your brain do? Start the anxiety program! That's why you're stuck in an endless loop.

You see, everytime:

- I started a new therapy;
- I started a new video course;
- I started reading a book;
- etc.

Every single time I had the following thoughts / mindset:

- Maybe this therapy/therapist can help me solve the problem / get rid of my anxiety
- Maybe this course can help me solve the problem / get rid of my anxiety
- Maybe this book can help me solve the problem / get rid of my anxiety

But I never found the solution. And now I know why. I always thought these methods would help me get rid of my problem (stopping the anxiety program). I was looking for the secret ingredient. So It doesn't really matter what kind of therapy you go through, what course you take or what book you read. If you think it's going to help you solve the problem then it simply will never help you. Because the problem is you trying to solve the problem!

In this book, you learn absolute nothing about how to get rid of your anxiety or how to solve the problem. You're going to learn how to stop trying to solve the problem.

This is the secret ingredient you've been looking for. This is the reason why you are stuck with anxiety or any mental problems for years or maybe even decades. This is the reason why nothing seems to work.

Important to remember: whatever you're going to do after reading this book, promise me you won't try to get rid of your anxiety. This will never work. It's the root cause of your anxiety.

9.1 What is your personal goal?

The purpose of this book is being "OK" with your thoughts, sensations, emotions and feelings and help you stop trying to get rid of them. But what is your personal goal? What do you want to achieve after applying everything in this book in practice? It's not about what you **don't** want but all about what you **do** want!

SILENCE

One of my personal goals:

When I went to sleep I always focused on my heart, feeling every beat. My anxiety was:

> "If I feel my heart beating, I'm unable to fall asleep."

As a result, every night before I went to sleep I focused on my heartbeat to check if I still felt my heart beating. You guessed the result, my heart just started beating even faster and I didn't fall asleep at all...

My personal goal would be that I'm "OK" that I feel my heartbeat and that I don't have to fall asleep right away. However, in this case, it's not about my heart beating but about the consequences of not being able to get enough sleep. My heartbeat prevented me from falling asleep, but what's the big deal? I was mainly afraid of not getting enough sleep and that I would be tired the next day. And that a lack of sleep would be bad for my body in the long run.

I had put enormous pressure on myself to fall asleep as soon as I got into bed. But I couldn't fall asleep because I could feel my heart beating all the time. The fact that I felt my heart beating was the result of my disaster scenarios (future predictions) about the consequences of poor sleep. So the actual goal for me would be to be "OK" with the fact that I'm tired the next day. Because once I accept that, it doesn't matter that I don't fall asleep right away. And in the end, there is no longer any reason to continuously check my heart rate.

So my personal goal was not:

> "I don't want to feel my heartbeat when I go to sleep"

My personal goal was:

Johan

> "It's "OK" that I am tired the next day" "My body can handle it"

What is your personal goal?

We'll use your personal goals in various assignments. So take the time to see what you really want. If you still think that your anxiety has to go away or that you don't want to feel X anymore, you're not in the right mindset yet. Recall the misery from Chapter six:

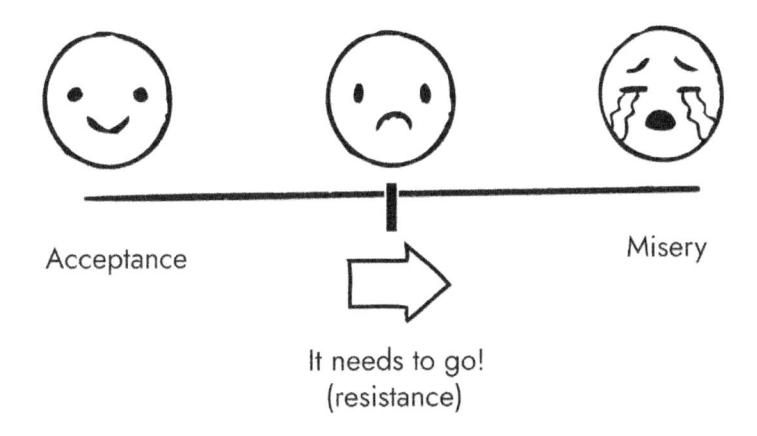

Acceptance — It needs to go! (resistance) — Misery

Realize that your goal can't be to get rid of your anxiety. The only possible outcome is misery.

Assignment: Write down your personal goal. Make your goals realistic and not too big. Stick to a maximum of two goals at first.

Think carefully about your actual anxiety. For example, that I couldn't sleep because of heart palpitations had nothing to do with palpitations, but that I would be tired the next day. Another example, people who continuously feel strange sensations around their heart are not afraid of these sensations, but that they'll have a heart attack and die. So they're afraid of death.

SILENCE

Try to look in detail at your anxiety. What exactly are you afraid of?

After you've written down your goals, can you imagine being OK with the things you fear? Just think about it for a second and notice what thoughts pop up and write them down. For example, someone that is afraid of having a heart attack might have thoughts like

> "How can I ever be OK with having a heart attack!?" "I don't want to die!"

Johan

Summary theme 1

In the first theme you've become acquainted with my experience of anxiety and panic. In addition, you're certainly not the only one with specific anxiety or panic complaints. There are literally hundreds of millions of people with the exact same problem. Your anxiety is not unique. It's even quite normal.

Sometimes it's difficult to explain to someone what you feel or think. Someone who's never experienced anxiety doesn't know exactly what you are thinking or feeling. Anxiety and love are quite close in terms of actions, ways of thinking and behavior. In both cases, you can't get something out of your head. Does someone not understand what you are thinking or feeling? Then try to explain that you are in love with someone and just can't get this person out of your mind no matter what you do.

Stop trying to solve your anxiety is the only long-term effective solution. Everything you can't accept will only result in misery. The only reason that your anxiety and panic rule your life is because you constantly resist it and are looking for a solution. A way to stop the anxiety program from running. But this solution does not exist. So you are getting stuck in an endless loop of ways trying to solve the problem.

Psychologists can help you solve anxieties. But many psychologists don't exactly know how anxiety works. Current treatment techniques have been lagging behind for years. In many cases, they give you medication right from the start while that's not necessary at all. Make the right decision for yourself by first sorting everything out. What do you expect from a treatment? Do you know what the consequences of medication are? Who will treat you? Did this person experience anxiety or panic attacks or did they just read about them in a book?

SILENCE

When talking to psychologists you always get a label. This label often contains the word "disorder". Like something is very wrong with you. That you have some kind of illness. There is absolutely nothing wrong with your brain or neurotransmitters. You have a disturbed thinking pattern. You're totally fine!

Finally, we looked at the main goal of this book and your personal goal. Your personal goal is very important. Anxiety will never go away. It's part of your body and mind. Therefore, take a good look at your personal goal. Focus on what you **do** want instead of what you **don't** want.

Assignments in theme 1:

- **Assignment:** Write down for yourself the positive things you get from your anxiety
- **Assignment:** Write down your personal goal in your notebook.

Johan

Theme 2: How does anxiety work in your body and mind?

In theme 2, we'll look at how anxiety works in your body and mind. Anxiety is a very important emotion for us as humans. Without this emotion, the human race would've been extinct a long time ago.

You're going to learn that your anxieties are just fantasy. Completely made up. Although at the moment it's probably controlling your life. You'll also learn what the difference is between anxiety and panic, how your brain works and what causes your anxiety and panic symptoms in the first place.

Chapter 10: How anxiety works in your body

Anxiety is regulated by the amygdala and is located in your brain. You're born with anxiety. And there's nothing you can do about that. But there is nothing wrong with that either. Without the amygdala, the human race would not even exist.

Did you know your amygdala can actually grow? When you have many anxious thoughts your amygdala goes into overdrive and actually grows. Producing even more anxious hormones and causing more and more anxious thoughts and behaviors.

As a child of anxious parents, you might learn certain anxious patterns. You notice how your parents react to certain situations. A child often imitates the behavior of their parents. So you can also subconsciously learn to be afraid of something because your parents react in a certain way. A personal example is my mother's interaction with my son and daughter. My mother is extremely concerned if my son or daughter trips or cries. I eventually started to notice that she was overly concerned while I thought "Let them cry, there is nothing wrong". It may well be that my parents also reacted to me in this way when I was a baby. It may well be that this behavior influenced me later in life.

Most of the time anxiety is conditioned. Meaning something happened and you conditioned your brain to be anxious about that situation. For example, as a child, you have no clue that a hot pan can hurt you. So you carelessly touch it sooner or later. But once you experience a hot pan that can burn your skin you quickly learn to never touch a hot pan again. Or when you had a severe car accident, you can condition your brain to be afraid of driving cars because it nearly killed you the last time.

Johan

You can also condition your brain to be anxious about no life-threatening situations. Like social anxiety. Millions of people suffer some form of social anxiety. Think of:

- Giving presentations;
- Talking to unknown people;
- Large groups of people in public spaces;
- Extreme discomfort with people you don't know.
- Etc.

But these are not life-threatening situations. You won't die giving a presentation in front of 100 people (although it feels like you're going to die...).

As you've read in my own story, I suffered from social anxiety. This was mainly out of a sense of shame. Other people weren't allowed to see me like that (with a blushing red face). Imagine if someone saw that my face would turn red. What would people think? Any time I was in a social situation, my amygdala kicked in fifth gear. My body was in full fight or flight mode while giving presentations or talking in large groups. As if I was attacked by ten wild tigers that didn't have food for weeks. Those were the conscious and unconscious signals that I passed on to my amygdala. The amygdala then activates all kinds of systems to protect me from danger. By indicating that I immediately had to run away from the situation. But I did not run away. Because you can't just run away while giving a presentation. What would people think of that...!

If a certain situation has made you anxious, there is a good chance that you will become anxious again the next time you encounter the same situation. And the more often this happens, the more anxious you become. It's a so-called self-fulfilling prophecy. Which means that what you think about actually happens. You think about a certain situation in advance and already know what the outcome will be. At least that's what you tell yourself. In my case, I was already nervous days before giving

SILENCE

a presentation. I predicted that I would be very nervous and my face would turn red during the presentation. But thinking about it like that made me nervous and red. <u>Not by giving the presentation but by the thoughts I had about it.</u>

Your amygdala's purpose is to protect you. Anxiety about flying and heights are the most normal things in the world. There is hardly anyone who doesn't feel any anxiety when they stare 100 meters into the depths. Because everyone knows "if I fall now I'm dead". And your amygdala knows that too.

If someone startles you by making a loud noise out of nowhere or jumping out of the bushes, this will trigger an automatic reaction. Not long ago we lived in the middle of the jungle. Surrounded by all kinds of dangers. Such as wild animals, snakes, tigers and so on. Then it's a good thing that your amygdala takes the lead and immediately enables you to react when you hear a loud noise or rustling in the bushes.

During anxious moments, a number of things happen in your body that are controlled by the amygdala:

- Your heart starts beating faster (so it can pump blood to the muscles faster);
- Your breathing increases to suck in more oxygen;
- Your pupils dilate so you can see more clearly;
- Your digestion is greatly slowed down;
- Your cortisol level rises;

All energy in your body is diverted to your muscles and all other non-vital functions are stopped. With the sole purpose that you can run away from a life-threatening situation as quickly as possible.

Austria 2010. I was on a skiing holiday with a group of friends. I had been single for a while at the time, so I slept alone for a number of years. During winter sports you often share a double

Johan

bed. I was sharing a bed with a friend. During the first night, I woke up in the middle of the night. I didn't know where I was anymore. At that moment I suddenly became aware that someone was lying next to me. My reaction was so intense that I was standing next to my bed completely awake within 0.01 seconds.

I could never consciously get out of bed that quickly. That's impossible. But because I consciously and unconsciously gave my amygdala a signal that I might be in danger, I was able to react extremely quickly to the situation. In this case, by jumping straight out of my bed in high alertness. In other words, my body was completely prepared to flee or fight.

Whether it concerns dangerous tigers in the jungle or giving a presentation in front of a hundred people, the reaction of your amygdala is exactly the same. But of course, it's a bit redundant to turn on this fight and flight system when giving a presentation in front of a hundred people. It feels like there are one hundred tigers in front of you, but in reality, nothing happens at all. However, that doesn't matter to the amygdala. As long as you see (how you think about the situation) this as a danger, the flight and fight system will be activated.

You can't turn off the amygdala. In fact, be glad you have an amygdala. You probably wouldn't be alive without it! Your amygdala only needs to learn that you won't be attacked by wild tigers while giving a presentation.

Look at your anxiety and your amygdala with admiration. That your amygdala does all this to protect you. Admire your anxiety. Your amygdala keeps you alive. If you didn't have an amygdala, you would have been run over by a car multiple times. It is not the situation or environment that makes you anxious. But how you think about it and are convinced that these thoughts are true.

SILENCE

Main concepts:

- Your amygdala protects you from danger;
- Your amygdala makes your body ready to fight or flee in anxietyful situations;
- You can control your amygdala with your thoughts.

Chapter 11: How anxiety works in Your Mind

Anxiety and panic attacks always start from:

- A thought;
- A sensation;
- An emotion;
- A feeling.

- **A thought could be:** "I need to give a presentation to 50 unknown people"
- **A sensation could be:** "You feel your heart skipping a few beats"
- **An emotion could be:** "The first time you experience an outburst of anger (tantrum)"
- **A feeling could be:** "You're feeling down last few days or weeks"

Thoughts, sensations, emotions and feelings are the most normal things in the world. Literally, everyone has to deal with this. Realize that there are billions of people who have the exact same sensations, emotions and thoughts that you experience. Many people with anxiety think they are the only one with super-specific thoughts or feelings. But it's much more common than you think.

People with anxiety don't think differently from people who don't **suffer** from anxious thoughts. Because suffering is the result of overthinking something. The difference is that people with anxiety make up subsequent catastrophic events. People without anxiety don't. And that has everything to do with cognitive thinking, which we discussed in theme 1. We start thinking about our thoughts, feelings, sensations and emotions.

SILENCE

The second step is **identifying** with them (believing them) and it goes down from there.

As a reminder: Without thinking about thoughts or feelings, anxiety, panic and depression can't exist.

A few years ago I became a father of a son. The first time I bathed my son, the following thought came to mind:

> "I can push him underwater and then he's gone…"

Of course, this is not a positive or pleasant thought. Only the thought is completely normal. I'm not a bad parent because I had such a thought. Probably this thought came to my mind because I'm also anxious to go underwater. Afraid that I can't get out and drown.

This particular thought had no effect on me. Because I know I would never deliberately put my son underwater. However, the same thought can cause a complete shock wave in someone else.

- "**What if** I stab him with this knife..?"
- "**What if** I throw him down the stairs..?"
- "**What if** I drown him in his bathtub..?"

What happens next is that this person starts thinking about these thoughts. These are always "What if…?" thoughts. What if thoughts are quickly followed by <u>disaster scenarios</u> or catastrophic events. Resistance against these thoughts and feelings are building up:

- "Did I really think I would push my son underwater…?"
- "I'm not supposed to have this thought at all…"
- "Do I want to hurt my son…?"

Johan

The negative attention to these thoughts causes you to build up <u>resistance</u>. You might tell yourself that you shouldn't think that way because otherwise, you're a bad parent. Or that maybe other people will think you're a bad parent. What would your partner think…? etc.

Now that you've been through all of this, you automatically connect to your feelings, thoughts, and sensations in that particular situation. There is a very good chance that the next time you encounter the same situation you'll look for the same feelings, thoughts and sensations. Not because you want to look them up, but because you don't want them ever again.

The next time I bathe my son, the same thought might come up again:

"I can now push him underwater and then he's gone…"

Suppose I had developed anxiety about these thoughts or situations, the thoughts often start <u>before</u> the situation happens:

- "What if I get those weird thoughts again.."
- "Disaster scenario: Could I really hurt him…?"
- "Disaster scenario: What if I actually do it…"
- "I don't dare bathe my son anymore…"

See what's happening here? Even before the situation arises, you start worrying about what might or might not happen. People without anxiety also have "what if" thoughts and disaster scenarios in their heads. They just don't look at it with negative attention. You can't build up resistance without negative attention.

Paying attention is therefore the most important link in stopping the anxiety program from running. Anxiety simply won't affect you if you don't give it negative attention (thinking about it in a

SILENCE

negative way). It's also important to realize that you can give attention in different ways. If you give negative attention to resistance it will grow. If you give it positive attention, the opposite happens.

You also have a way to respond to fear using an automatic system called instinct. Suppose your baby suddenly slips out of your hands and goes underwater. The first reflex you have is to lift your baby out of the bath as quickly as possible without thinking about it. But you can also become frozen. In acute anxious or panic situations, you have zero control over how you react.

What does this look like visually:

Johan

Thoughts
Sensations
Emotions
Feelings

Cognitive Thinking

Act out of Instinct

Automatic Reflex

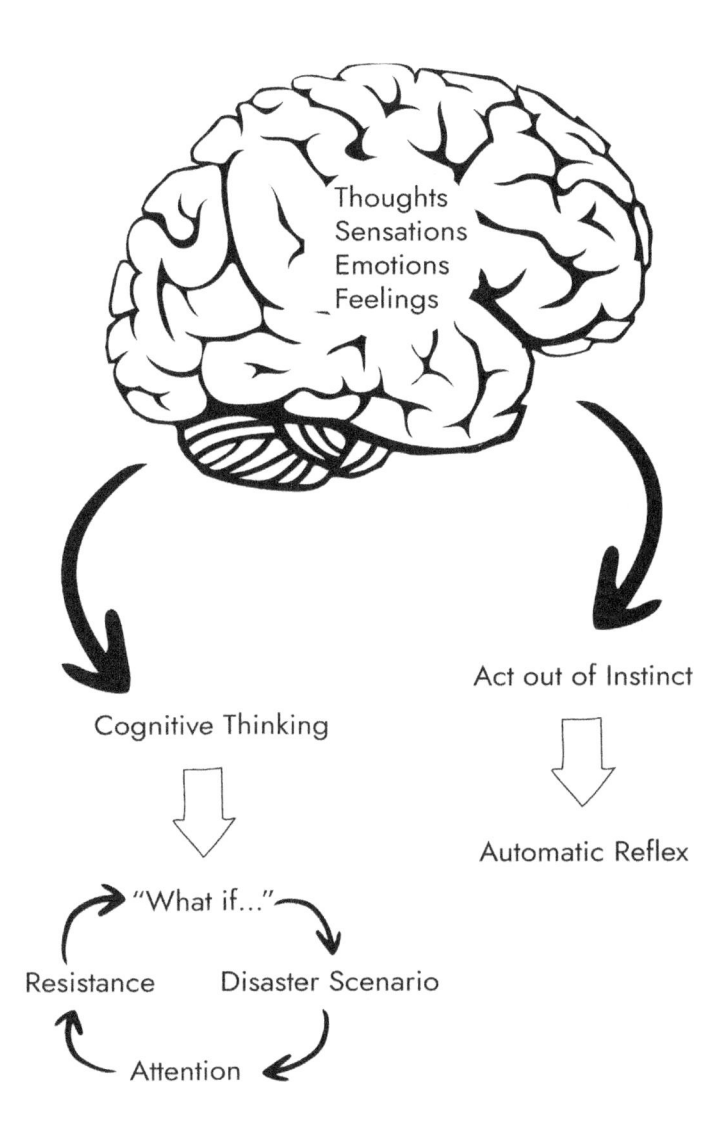

"What if..."
Resistance   Disaster Scenario
Attention

The process of anxiety and panic can be divided into two parts. The cognitive part and the instinctive part.

You have no influence over the instinctive part. Each person reacts in his own way to a certain situation. One person is

SILENCE

frozen, the other runs away. This system only activates in unexpected anxious situations. The situation happens so quickly that you hardly have time to think about it. And that's a good thing because if you need to think about the situation first you might already be dead.

Consider the example of my holiday in Austria. I had the thought that something was completely wrong because someone was lying next to me in bed while I had almost always slept alone in recent years. Then my instinct took over and I was wide awake standing next to my bed within 0.01 seconds. That was not a conscious action. So my automatic response is to flee.

Some other examples of instinctive action:

- You end up with your car on the verge (reflex, you throw the steering wheel)
- You unexpectedly encounter a bear in the woods (you freeze or run away very quickly)
- Someone gives you an unexpected shock (you scream, freeze or jump away)
- Someone scares you, you start to run away or freeze and scream.
- Etc.

You can't influence your response. Because the danger is so acute that your body intervenes. If you have to think carefully about what is actually going on, you might be too late.

In the cognitive part, you are thinking. You are thinking about thought, sensation, emotion, or feeling. You get "what if" thoughts and you make up disaster scenarios. Disaster scenarios are always negative, so you'll pay extra attention to them. Because you don't want this disaster scenario to come true. The more negative attention you give to the disaster scenario (the disaster scenario must not come true at all costs), the more you will resist. Then more "what if.." thoughts and disaster scenarios pass by. And that's when the anxiety program kicks in:

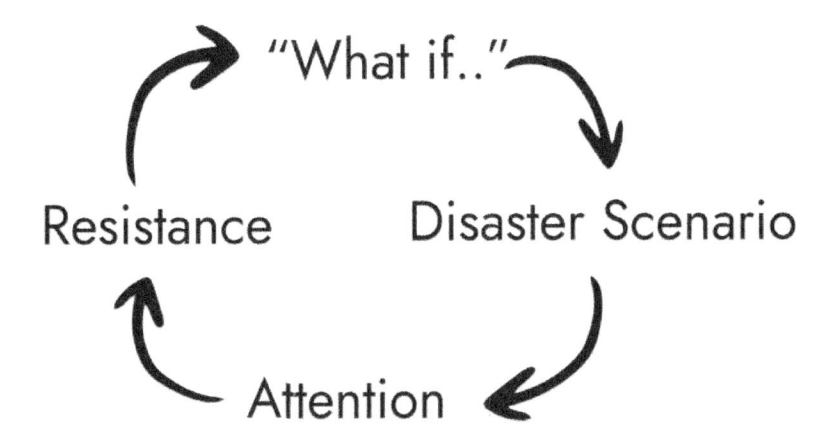

Resistance → "What if.." → Disaster Scenario → Attention → Resistance

- **What if…..?**
- What will happen (**disaster scenario**)?
- **Attention**: This (the disaster scenario) must be avoided at all costs.
- **Resist**: You'll do everything you can to prevent the disaster scenario from happening.

Resistance often consists of control:

- "I don't want to think about this.."
- "I don't want to feel this sensation.."
- "I don't want to feel that way."
- "It has to go.."

You're going to check whether that thought or sensation is still present. For example, you check whether that weird sensation around your heart is still there. Or you're going to check if you still feel bad. But you don't want that sensation near your heart because it might indicate a heart attack. And you certainly don't want to feel bad all day. So the sensation has to go and you have

SILENCE

to feel good again. Because you want to control (resist) the sensation and your feelings, it will only make the complaints worse.

The anxiety you suffer from always comes from the cognitive part. An emotion, thought, sensation or feeling is always **neutral**. <u>It's our thoughts about them that make them a positive or negative experience.</u>

This circle of "what if..." thoughts, disaster scenarios, attention and resistance can eventually result in a panic attack. You go through this circle so quickly and build up so much resistance that at some point it's no longer sustainable. A panic attack is an accumulation of anxious thoughts, feelings, and emotions. A panic attack is 100% anxiety. A panic attack is the maximum limit of anxiety that your mind and body can handle.

The more you think about your thoughts or emotions (in a negative way) the deeper you get stuck in this process. You'll resist even more because your complaints seem to be getting worse. You get anxious thoughts more often, a panic attack more often or that sensation becomes intensely present every single day. Then you think about it again. And before you know it you are completely stuck in the anxiety program and it won't stop running.

And now you know why. The anxiety program won't stop running because you are trying to stop it from running. You are trying to get rid of your sensations and thoughts. But you are actually giving your mind the instruction to find a solution for your problem so you mind starts the anxiety program. Does it start to make sense?

In theme three we will try to prevent the anxiety program from running with different techniques.

Johan

The example of giving my son a bath starts with a thought. With a physical sensation, the process works exactly the same:

1. You feel a sensation;
2. You start thinking about It in a negative way "**What if**...";
3. **Disaster scenario:** "There might be something wrong with my heart. I'm going to die!";
4. You start giving extra **attention** to the sensation because you don't want to die!;
5. You build up **resistance** against the sensation (as long as the sensation is still there, something must be wrong!);
6. You continuously check whether the sensation is still there;
7. Yes, it's still there! This is not good... Then you return to step 2 to repeat the cycle over and over.

A personal example:

At one point I felt a sensation around my heart region. A stabbing sensation in the chest. I got hooked almost immediately with thoughts and attention:

- "What is this..."
- "This is not good..."
- "Something is wrong with my heart..."

Pretty soon the anxiety program started running (my mind is trying to protect me) and I was checking (resisting) a hundred times a day if those weird sensations in my chest were still there. Because I gave it so much attention, the sensations became very noticeable. My sensations became more intense by the day and I started to sweat. Because I had read somewhere (on the internet...) that you get pain in your arms during or just before a heart attack, I started checking my arms to notice any pain. And of course, I started to feel pain in my arms! In the end, I was so extremely focused on not wanting a heart attack, I had all the symptoms of a heart attack:

SILENCE

- Pain in the chest;
- Pain in the arms;
- Sweating a lot...

I was 100% convinced that I would have a heart attack and drop dead! But nothing happened...

When the complaints didn't go away (in other words, I kept thinking about it), my doctor gave me a machine to check my heart for the next 24 hours. The results were examined by a cardiovascular specialist. After investigation, it turned out that nothing was wrong at all. So I was driving myself completely crazy with thoughts and extreme attention to sensations that weren't caused by any heart problems. The sensations were real and I felt them. But they were only there because I was afraid of them, didn't want them and had an extreme focus on them.

The stabbing sensation in my chest was real. The pain in my arms and the sweating was just a result of anxiety. But in my mind, these were all indications of a heart attack. And that makes anxiety so incredibly difficult. Because it all feels so real but it's not. It's just the **consequence** of your behavior and thoughts, not reality. It's fantasy.

In this specific case, the anxiety program stopped running after I received the results from the doctor.

"I was checked by a specialist. Then it's ok"

After I got the results, I never felt the sensation again. So what actually happened:

- My "What if..." thoughts are debunked by the doctor. I trusted the result 100%;
- Because I no longer had "What if there is something wrong with my heart" thoughts, there was no more

disaster scenario "I'm going to have a heart attack, I'm going to die...";
- Because there was no longer a disaster scenario, I could no longer pay attention to it;
- Because I no longer paid attention to the disaster scenario, there was no longer any need to check (resist) whether I felt weird sensations around my heart;
- The anxiety program stopped running. "What if..." thoughts about my heart didn't occur at all after that.

In my case, I trusted the results from the doctor. But there are also people who don't trust the results of the specialist:

- **What if** the doctor didn't look closely?
- Did he check everything properly?
- **What if** he missed something...?
- I still feel the sensation....

And then anxiety can take a very nasty turn. Because when can you be 100% sure about anything?

Exactly the same thing can happen with a feeling and an emotion. Suppose you've been feeling a bit depressed in recent weeks, don't feel like doing anything, etc. At some point, you become aware of that. And at that very moment you start thinking about it:

- "I've actually been feeling down for a while..."
- "Why do I feel this way...?"
- "What if I am mildly depressed...?"

Everyone has had these thoughts or feelings at one time or another. You usually get over it. Until you start giving it too much attention. At some point, you're checking daily and wondering why you feel this way. Then the resistance "I want to feel good again" or "I don't want to feel this" starts.

SILENCE

Depression goes a little deeper than anxiety and panic. But even if you struggle with depression it's important to feel everything you feel and think. No matter how negative it is. If you build up resistance to those feelings, you'll only get more depressed thoughts and feelings. In that respect, depression works exactly the same as anxiety and panic. Exactly the reason that cognitive behavioral therapy is given as the primary treatment for anxiety, panic and depression. In other words, learn to think differently about what you think and feel.

It's also possible that your own behavior creates more disaster scenarios without realizing it. For example, you've been feeling tired for a while and therefore decide to stop exercising for the next few weeks. After making this decision your condition deteriorates even further and you feel even more tired. You then link this to the thoughts and feelings you already had and see it as confirmation. While in reality you only became more tired because you stopped exercising.

11.1 There is no such thing as 100% certainty

Almost everyone with anxiety is looking for validation. Confirmation that the disaster scenario does not happen. My personal example of sensations around the heart region can be viewed in several ways. My anxiety was gone after I was checked by a doctor. But there are also people who don't trust the result.

> **"What if** the doctor missed something?"

A new disaster scenario is created after the doctor has checked everything. What is the consequence of this new scenario? That the doctor missed something and you could still have a heart attack at any time. The result is that you still give attention to the sensations in your heart region. Search and you will find. Of course, the weird sensations are still there. The anxiety program is still running. The only difference is that new disaster scenarios have now been invented by your mind.

Johan

It's possible that the doctor missed something. That happens very sporadically. When you have these kinds of thoughts you're looking at your anxiety with an extreme magnifying glass. The simple fact is that no one can check whether you are 100% healthy. At the 2021 European Football Championship, Christian Eriksen fell down on the pitch. He went into cardiac arrest. While the heart of this top athlete is screened every year and is in tip-top condition. Despite all the screenings, he still had a heart attack. Whatever your anxiety, there is no 100% certainty that your disaster scenario will never come true.

Always try to view your anxiety from reality. What makes sense? Does it make sense that you have a high chance of becoming a millionaire if you participate in the lottery? No. Does it make sense if you live quite healthy that you get a heart attack out of nowhere? No.

In fact, anxiety usually works the other way around. Someone who's afraid of getting into an accident while driving will pay much more attention to traffic and will therefore be less likely to get into an accident. Someone who is afraid of getting sick will generally eat much healthier foods. Can you 100% rule out that you'll never have an accident? No, because if someone else isn't paying attention you can still have an accident. Can you 100% rule out that you'll never get sick because you eat super healthy? No, getting sick has to do with much more variables than just eating healthy.

Try to abandon the search for 100% certainty. No one has all the answers to your questions. That's what makes life so beautiful. Wouldn't it be boring if you knew the answer to every question?

Assignment: Can you convince yourself 100% that your disaster scenario can't come true if you do X?

SILENCE

In other words, if you do X, you are 100% sure that your disaster scenario will never come true. Is there a way or is there always uncertainty?

Write it down and discuss it with a friend or family member. Your goal is to convince them that your disaster scenario can't happen if you do X and they have to 100% agree.

Chapter 12: Your anxiety is fantasy!

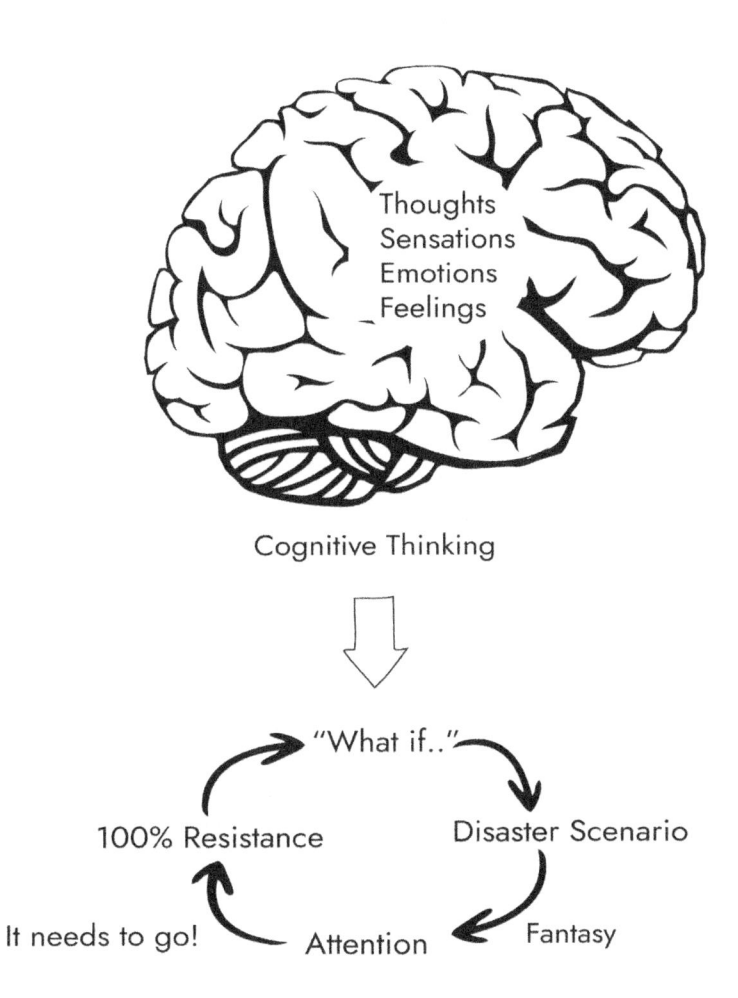

Thoughts
Sensations
Emotions
Feelings

Cognitive Thinking

"What if.."

Disaster Scenario

Fantasy

Attention

It needs to go!

100% Resistance

All thoughts that arise from "What if…" and subsequent disaster scenarios are fantasy. Completely made up by your mind. All you do is try to predict the future. If I told you that

SILENCE

there is someone who can predict the future, would you believe me? No, most likely not. There is no one in the world who can predict what will happen tomorrow. But you still think otherwise. Has your anxiety ever come true?

Countless times I have tried to predict my future with "What if..." thoughts. But they never really came true. It's very important to know which thoughts or situations you're trying to predict. Your anxiety has a bit more depth to it than you might think. A personal example: I was afraid of having a panic attack while driving. As soon as I got into the car I was already panicking.

"What if I have a panic attack while driving...?"

It wasn't the panic attack I was actually afraid of. But for the consequence of the panic attack. I was afraid of losing control and having an accident.

My anxiety "What if I have a panic attack while driving...?" actually became true. So you could say that the anxiety is not a fantasy because it really happened. Only in this case, it's not so much about the panic attack, however annoying, but the anxiety of causing an accident. Do you completely lose control during a panic attack so you can cause an accident? No, that has never happened to me and it has never happened to other people with panic attacks either. So while I was experiencing the maximum anxiety my body and mind can handle (a panic attack is 100% anxiety), I was still 100% in control. If I wanted to I could drive to the emergency lane and get out of the car. The chance that your anxiety will come true is so incredibly small and sometimes even literally impossible that you can label it as fantasy.

You can compare a disaster scenario with an advertisement for a random lottery. Extreme focus is placed on winning a big bag of money. Because so much focus is placed on the big bag of money (who doesn't want to become a millionaire...?), you lose focus on the other side of the story. The chance that you win the main prize in the lottery is statistically 0. You have a higher chance of a plane falling from the sky and crashing into your house. Yet many millions of people play the lottery and hope (against their better judgment) that they'll win a big prize.

It works exactly the same with anxiety. There is an extreme focus on a negative disaster scenario, but the chance that this scenario will actually become true is near zero.

12.1 Resistance

The "What if..." thoughts and disaster scenarios are fantasy. The attention that occurs while trying to suppress these thoughts, feelings and sensations creates resistance. There is no one in the world who thinks at his first panic attack:

> "That felt good, give me some more!"

Rather the opposite. I never want to feel this again!!! And so the building of resistance against these emotions and feelings begins. However, this will only increase the severity and panic attacks will happen more often.

That is why anxiety, panic and depression can be very difficult to accept. You try to do well. You try to protect yourself. You do everything to feel good. And that's also a very logical way of thinking. In practice, however, it works exactly the other way around. Something you don't want to think about keeps haunting your mind all the time. And everything you do want to think about, you let go automatically. That's how your brain works.

You don't have to do something to let it go, **you need to stop doing something to let it go**!

SILENCE

A good example is love. You like someone you met so much that you can't stop thinking about this person. You want him/her to like you back so much that you become completely blindsided. You no longer see negative things. That one person is just totally amazing. While that is not realistic at all since you don't know that person that well yet.

With anxiety, it works the other way around. You only see negative things while there are also a lot of positive things in your life. Probably anxiety is one of the few negative things in your life. But your resistance to anxiety is so great that it seems as if that's the only thing that interests you right now and needs to be solved immediately.

So start living your life <u>regardless</u> of your anxiety! You don't need to solve your problems first before you can start living. That exact mindset is one of the root causes of your problems!

Do you know what's the biggest joke of all? If you have a realistic look at what is actually happening, you are resisting a fantasy that you have made up yourself!

Johan

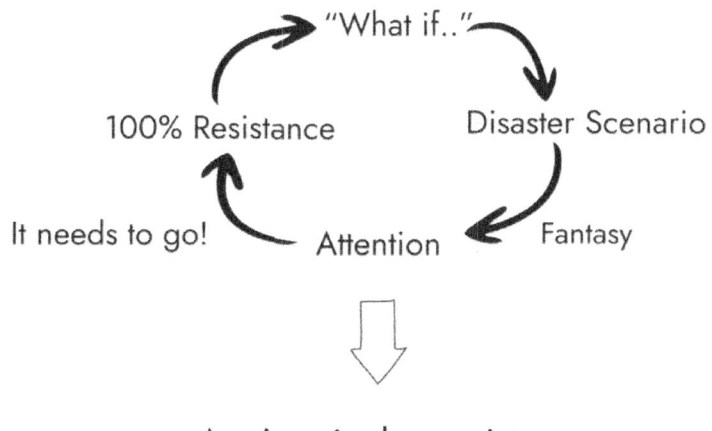

```
        → "What if.."
   ⟲                 ⟱
100% Resistance    Disaster Scenario
   ⬆                 ⟲
It needs to go!  ← Attention ←  Fantasy
              ⬇
```

Anxiety is the resistance against your made-up fantasy!

12.2 When your fantasy comes true

One of my anxieties was that I couldn't sleep well due to stress and heart palpitations. I had bad nights for months and even years. Waking up in the middle of the night. Not getting back to sleep etc. I have no insomnia or whatever. I slept eight hours a night for over 30 years. Only because I had an extreme focus on my heart and forcing myself to sleep well, my sleep pattern deteriorated very vastly. So you could say that the fantasy that I would not be able to get quality sleep due to stress and heart palpitations came true.

In this case, it was not so much about the heart palpitations and the stress but about the consequence. What's so bad about not sleeping well? That has to do with my anxiety about my health. You've probably heard or read that you always need at least eight hours of sleep to recover properly and stay healthy. That was so imprinted in my mind that sleeping badly was not an

SILENCE

option for me. As if after a week of bad sleep I wouldn't be able to perform at all, would get sick and then die in the worst case.

But you guessed it, that didn't happen. Of course, I was a bit tired. But I could work fine, exercise and do everything I normally did. I was just a little tired. My disaster scenarios were not related to stress or heart palpitations but to the consequence of not having enough sleep. In other words, it might as well have been another bodily sensation that kept me awake.

The solution in this case was not to get rid of the palpitations or stress. But to accept that I would be tired the next day and that I don't need eight hours of sleep to function. I had a hard time telling myself this. I didn't believe my own words. Until something happened:

I felt very panicky for a few days. I was scanning my body for weird sensations. But especially trying to get rid of the panicky feeling. I was totally stressed. In addition, during the day I was terrified of the night. Afraid that I would lie awake all night worrying etc. Of course that night I was lying awake fully stressed and worrying.... That night was one of the worst in my life. Nevertheless, I was not tired the next day. In fact, even well into the evening of the next day, I didn't feel tired at all. In other words, if I had really slept that badly I would have been tired this late at night. Only then did the realization really sink in that my thoughts are simply not true. Of course, the thoughts were still present in the nights that followed. But I became pretty good at convincing myself that these thoughts were complete nonsense.

> "I had one of the worst nights of my life. Yet, I was not even tired the next day. How can that be?"

And just like my fear of causing an accident when having a panic attack while driving didn't come true. I did have panic attacks while driving, but it never caused an accident. I did feel weird sensations in my chest and had all the symptoms of a heart attack but I never had a heart attack. My face turned red in social situations but I could never know what other people actually thought of me. It was all inside my mind. Just as your disaster scenarios are most likely just a fantasy.

I also experienced anxiety about something that was very real. I'll tell you more about this later on.

12.3 You are not your thoughts

It's important to realize that your thoughts are not yours. **You are the observer of thoughts**. Thoughts are just a construct of the mind to help you live your life. Give yourself a moment and try to stop all thinking. Pick an object in your room or outside like a tree. Give that object your full attention for a few minutes but without thinking about the object. Just observe it.

Did you notice that without any thought, you are still there? You are very alive without any thoughts. Thoughts are just words played in your head created by your mind. Like someone else is talking to you. And it's up to the real you to believe those thoughts, identify with them or let them be.

When the thoughts came back that I was going to sleep badly and would be tired again the next day with all the consequences, I said to myself:

> "I had the worst night of my life yesterday and I wasn't even tired the next day. I don't believe this nonsense anymore. I don't care anymore"

Since then I no longer care whether I sleep well or not. The above was the definitive breakthrough of this anxiety. I broke through the fantasy and with that, there was no longer any need for resistance.

SILENCE

That's why it's important to look for evidence. <u>Is it really true what you think?</u> In my case, I bought a fitness tracker that could measure my sleeping pattern and heart rate. And as it turned out, I slept eight hours almost every night... So I didn't sleep that bad at all. Therefore, take a very good look at your disaster scenario. What are you really afraid of? What happens when the disaster scenario becomes a reality? And the big question, has that ever happened?

When you learn to create a little distance between your thoughts and reality, you'll notice that your thoughts are just words passing by. They have zero meaning in reality. The only thing that's real is this moment right now. Right now reading these words. There is nothing more in life than just this moment. The future does not exist. Only this exact moment exists and everything else is just a construct of your mind. And when you realize this, your thoughts can't have any control over you. But this does not happen overnight and you need to practice this.

Assignment: Answer the following questions for yourself and write them down:

- What's the worst-case scenario that could happen?
- What's the real consequence of your disaster scenario?
- Has that ever happened?
- Are you still there, alive and alert even if you have zero thoughts?

Johan

Chapter 13: When there truly is something wrong

When you're afraid of sensations in your body, you pay a lot of attention to these sensations. As a result, the sensations become sensitive to your attention. The sensation will become more intense and present. So you might think that this sensation is real. You really feel the sensation but only because you pay attention to it.

It's important to realize that these sensations can be fantasy. And that makes the anxiety of physical sensations difficult because you do feel something in your body. But not all sensations are fantasy. How do you know when your sensations are real or fantasy?

There is a big difference between sensations that are already present and sensations that you create by paying attention to them. It's therefore quite possible that your heart actually beats faster or skips a few beats due to a medical cause. Or simply because your body reacts to food or some other external cause.

Personally, I suffer from tinnitus. It's in my family. Tinnitus is an ear condition that causes constant ringing in your ears. The cause is unknown. You can imagine that this can drive you completely crazy. For some people, it's so bad that they request euthanasia. It's a terrible disease.

At this moment, I also hear a ringing in my ear. This sensation is real. I actually have a ringing in my ear. But I only hear it when I pay attention to it. However, there was a time when I first discovered this ringing and I started to worry. **What if** this ringing in my ears would be there forever?

SILENCE

Now that you know how the anxiety program works, you can probably guess what happened next. My disaster scenario was:

> "What if I keep hearing that ringing in my ears forever?"
> —> "I can't live with that…"

So what did I do? Resisting the ringing in my ears. Checking every day if I still had a ringing in my ears. Of course, I still had a ringing in my ears! I started paying more attention to it. The ringing only got worse. I gave it so much attention that sounds even started to hurt my ears. My ears became so hypersensitive due to extreme attention to the ringing in my ear that I developed all kinds of pains. I tried everything to get rid of the ringing in my ears. Do you think that helped?

Exactly the reason why blind people can hear so well. They don't suddenly have highly developed hearing, but give all their attention to their hearing because they can't see. Then you automatically hear things that you would never hear otherwise.

There are many people with chronic pain complaints. While doctors can't find anything. If doctors can't find anything, this could very well indicate an attention problem. If you wake up every day in pain, it's a sincere question to check with yourself whether you immediately pay attention to it or whether you are actually in pain. My tinnitus was so bad that my hearing had become hypersensitive and literally hurt. Right now, I am no longer bothered by the ringing. I can't hear it anymore. The only difference is that I used to give the ringing an extreme amount of attention by wishing it away and now I don't care at all.

This is an example of a sensation where something is actually going on. But your mind is very capable of introducing sensations that are not real. I also experienced this.

Around 2015 I went to a festival party with some friends. I used ecstasy for the first time of my life and a few days later I woke up dizzy. I immediately started worrying that ecstasy must be the cause of this because I never felt dizzy this way. Also, after some Googling (bad idea when having anxiety...) I found out I had too much ecstasy according to my weight. Disaster scenario created:

> "**What if** the ecstasy has affected my brain and **I will be dizzy forever**!?"

Since that thought, I have literally been dizzy for many months 24/7. Because all my attention went to "not wanting to be dizzy". It's also very annoying and irritating. It has to go.

I do think I was really dizzy the first few days. All those months after that I "made up" my own dizziness by giving it extreme attention. When I finally stopped paying attention to the dizziness, I was no longer dizzy. So I was really dizzy but not for a medical reason. In other words, I was perfectly fine. Only my "what if" and disaster scenarios caused dizziness.

There is a very fine line between actual sensations and "made-up" sensations. Believe me, you can talk yourself into every sensation you want and think it's real. But how do you know if something is actually going on or if you're paying too much attention to it?

You can test this with an attention exercise. This can be a conscious exercise but also unconscious. A conscious exercise could be a body scan. With a body scan, you consciously listen to your body. If you go to your sensation with full attention and give it 100% attention in a positive way and you don't feel anything? Then there is most likely nothing wrong. However, if you are afraid of something, the biggest problem is to allow the sensation to just be. An unconscious exercise would be better in that case. That is quite difficult in practice because how are you going to do an exercise unconsciously?

SILENCE

For example, when you exercise. If you exercise intensively, you almost always have to give all your full attention to what you're doing. Think of a situation where you were not concerned with your anxiety or sensation at all. Did you still notice any weird sensations?

A personal example of an unconscious event:

I remember that I was dizzy all day. I was constantly checking if I was dizzy while cycling. At one point I ran into an old friend. We got into a conversation and spent 30 minutes catching up on anything and everything. Meanwhile, I was <u>subconsciously</u> no longer concerned with my dizziness. I was busy talking and was no longer dizzy at all! Until after the conversation I suddenly noticed **<u>consciously</u>** that I was not dizzy for the entire conversation. While I've been suffering from it all day every day for the last weeks and months. So apparently I'm only dizzy if I don't want it and giving it a lot of negative attention. But after I consciously noticed that my dizziness was gone, I automatically went back to checking if it was still gone. With the following thoughts:

> "Hey, how is that possible? I wasn't dizzy at all for 30 minutes!. How did I do that? I wasn't thinking about it. Ok, so just don't think about it! How am I not going to think about something?"

And for the rest of the day and the next few weeks I was dizzy again...

These thought patterns are the paradox of anxiety. **You can't consciously not think about something.** So you can't consciously check in the moment that you are no longer anxious. That's just impossible. That's not how your mind works. The only thing you can consciously do is let it go or let it be there without judgment. So the next weeks and months I got stuck in figuring out how to not pay attention to my dizziness. I probably don't have to tell you I never found the answer.

Suppose I had gone to the doctor with my dizziness, would they have found anything? Not in a million years. There was nothing physically wrong with me. If I got stuck in this mindset I could literally be dizzy for the rest of my life with no doctor or physician ever finding anything.

Everything that is anxiety-related will not manifest itself if you're not consciously thinking about it. That's simply impossible. I never was dizzy when I was not thinking about it. Because thinking about it (which is the root cause of literally any anxiety, panic or depression) caused my dizziness.

There are millions of people that feel physical sensations and think they have cancer, get a heart attack or get sick and die. While that can happen, chances are you are perfectly healthy. But to make sure, always check with a doctor so you can rule out any medical causes. Also, food and drinks can cause many physical sensations. So if you're sensitive to physical sensations, first figure out if they are real by doing some attention exercises like a body scan. Second, try to think of a situation where you were 100% distracted. Did you still feel the sensations when you were 100% distracted?

Chapter 14: What is a panic attack?

Now you know how anxiety works. But what is a panic attack? Panic is simply the maximum anxiety your body and mind can handle. Panic is 100% anxiety. Panic arises from anxious thoughts, feelings or sensations that become so bad that you don't know what to do anymore and panic.

When you have a panic attack for the first time, you have no idea what's going on. All kinds of weird sensations, feelings and emotions come up. Loss of control, afraid that something will happen or that you will die. Those are certainly not pleasant feelings.

It's also common for people to become afraid of a panic attack. You are completely overwhelmed by your first panic attack that you don't want to go through this again. Then you build up anxiety about anxiety.

Johan

Thoughts
Sensations
Emotions
Feelings

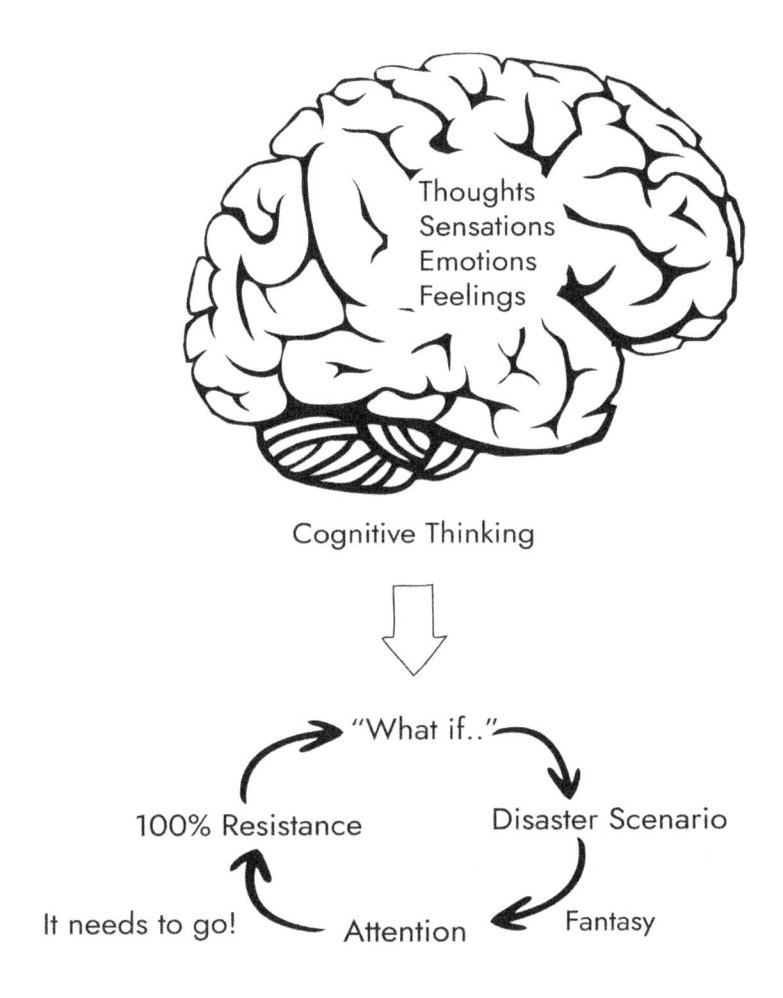

Cognitive Thinking

"What if.."
100% Resistance → Disaster Scenario
It needs to go! ← Attention ← Fantasy

Anxiety and panic go through the exact same steps. The only difference is that panic builds up so much resistance against thoughts, sensations, emotions, and feelings that there is no other option than a panic attack. So you could say that a panic attack is 100% resistance. 100% anxiety is 100% resisting thoughts, feelings and emotions.

With moderate anxiety you go through the same steps, only the resistance is not big enough to cause a panic attack. A panic

SILENCE

attack can also come on very quickly or build up very slowly. It's quite possible to be anxious all day, build up a little bit more resistance each hour and eventually have a panic attack at the end of the day.

An example of how panic can start:

1) Anxiety of having another panic attack (in a certain situation).
2) Disaster thoughts: "I'm going to have a panic attack while driving..."
3) The resistance starts even before getting in the car.
4) Attention and resistance go up to 100% once driving the car: "Here it comes again..NOOOOO."

Because you don't want to have a panic attack while driving, you will pay extra attention when you are in the car. Because the panic attack should absolutely not come while driving because then something will happen (you cause an accident and you die).

You try to push away feelings, sensations and thoughts at all costs. You enter the anxiety program and it starts running in a loop. Sometimes this happens so fast that you don't even realize what's happening.

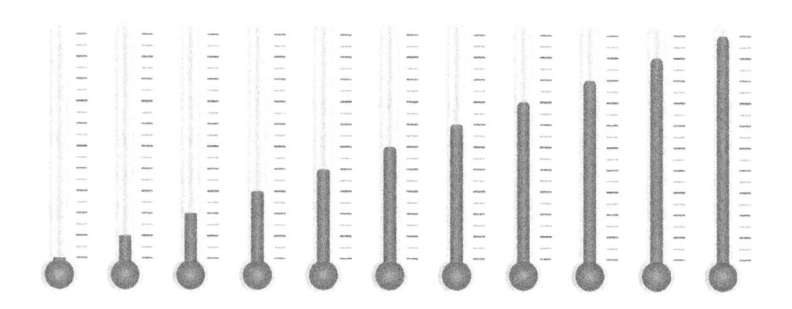

Johan

Anxiety is like a thermometer going from 0 to 100 degrees. Where 100 degrees is panic (100% anxiety). But this applies to any emotion. You can also be happy and cheerful on a scale of 0 - 100. Only a happy emotion will automatically make you go up to 100 degrees without resistance. Have you ever resisted a happy emotion?

I can think of a few situations. Think of a funny situation but since everyone around you is dead serious so it wasn't appropriate to burst out laughing. Good luck holding back your laughter. But also realize that you're doing the exact same thing with your anxiety and panic. Anxiety is no different from any other emotion. The only reason why you suffer is because you are limiting anxiety because you don't want it. If you limit happy emotions, the same thing will happen. It's almost impossible to hold back your laugh when something is really funny. A perfect example is the next video. It's about four guys in a car singing a song. The only thing they **can't do** is laugh. Let's see how that works out... ohh and when watching this video, you can't laugh either. Challenge accepted?

https://www.youtube.com/watch?v=WHbdJWbeZmc

They are resisting an emotion just like you are resisting your anxiety. It doesn't matter what emotion you resist, it always has to come out. In the case of the guys in the car, they burst into laughter eventually. In the case of anxiety, you'll end up in a panic attack eventually. How hard was it to keep in your laughter while watching the video?

Someone with anxiety always starts to resist at a certain point. If that point is reached, then (according to your fantasy) you have a problem and your anxiety comes true so you start resisting. And the ultimate resistance (100%) always ends up in a panic attack. And although it's very scary, nothing can happen. It's not like your body can't handle 100% anxiety because then you

SILENCE

would die. Your body and mind can perfectly handle a panic attack.

Main concepts:

- Panic is 100% anxiety
- 100% anxiety is 100% resisting thoughts, feelings, sensations or emotions
- You can't put a limit to any emotion <u>without</u> consequences

Johan

Chapter 15: The limit of your anxiety and breaking the resistance

Every emotion has a limit. This limit is normally always 100%. You can't experience more anxiety than a panic attack. Considering a panic attack is 100% anxiety. People with anxiety put a limit on their thoughts and feelings. These people are allowed to feel a maximum of 80 degrees anxiety. Others put a limit at 50 degrees. Your anxiety can reach a certain limit and above that limit, your resistance starts. The further you get above the limit, the harder you will resist.

Suppose you have social anxiety and get a red face in social situations. The thermometer can't exceed 80 degrees during a social interaction with the cashier in the supermarket, because then you'll get a red face. However, during a presentation where all eyes are on you, you set the limit at 30 degrees because now many more people can see your face. So it's almost inevitable that you'll get a red face. But if you are alone in the bathroom at home, the thermometer can rise to 100 degrees and you don't even care.

Social anxiety is for most people much worse in larger groups of people versus just talking to a single person. So the limit of their anxiety changes according to the situation. But they also experience situations where they have no limits. The only difference is that when you are alone in your bathroom at home, no disaster scenario exists. So you can't build resistance. The worst case scenario of someone blushing is that they are afraid that other people will see it and that other people will judge it. There is no one else in the bathroom when you're home alone. So the disaster scenario can never come true. There is no one there to judge your red face. Consequently, you

SILENCE

have zero resistance against the red face. That's why it's <u>literally impossible to consciously blush.</u> Just try it yourself. It doesn't matter if you suffer from blushing or not. Try to deliberately get a red face by thinking about it.

An example of how much influence your thoughts have:

Suppose you suffer from social anxiety. I tell you to give an online presentation to 150 people. These people all come together in Zoom or Microsoft Teams, but you can't see them live because everyone's webcam is turned off. Meanwhile, I asked these 150 people to take a break during the presentation. But you don't know that. I'll give a short introduction and then give you time to speak. What happens?

You're super nervous because you <u>think</u> 150 people are dead silent waiting for your presentation. While in reality, you talk to a screen that no one looks at or listens to because everyone is on break. Meanwhile, your anxiety limit is reached, you might start forgetting lines, get a red face or are stumbling over words.

The limit and the resistance can very well differ per situation. And you'll certainly have noticed that your anxiety is never exactly the same. Even if you are in the exact same situation. I've often experienced that my face turned red during the checkout in the supermarket, but only a day later I did not get a red face at all.

A lot of people have trouble allowing certain emotions and breaking through the resistance. This has nothing to do with anxiety. For example, it can also be about anger or sadness. In general, it's always "negative" emotions that people try to limit. By limit, I mean:

> "I may feel emotion X, but more than X is not allowed because then X will happen"

Suppose you put a limit on the emotion of joy. You can be happy and cheerful up to 50%, but you can't exceed that limit. Would that be something you would like? That you can only be 50% happy at all times? Is that even possible? Now imagine having to live like this your entire life. That you should always suppress your emotion of joy. Then you can never burst out laughing again. You always have to hold back. That doesn't really sound like something you'd want, right?

It works exactly the same with anxiety. People with anxiety put a limit on an emotion. This limit determines how much they are allowed to feel and think before resisting starts. Consequence? Anxiety complaints! Weird sensations, thoughts and emotions. You can't impose a limit on anxiety without consequences. Just as well that you can't put a limit on the emotion of joy without consequences. As you experienced in the video with the guys in the car.

Incidentally, it's not bad at all that you put a limit on emotions. It's not the goal to allow every emotion 100%. That's not realistic. You just have to decide where to set the limit. And you have to ask yourself what you will do if the emotion goes over the limit. Because that's going to happen sooner or later.

Assignment: Think about your own anxiety symptoms. What are you afraid of? In what situation does that manifest itself? And what is the limit you put on anxiety in that situation? When are you going to resist? Now that you think about it, do you also notice that your limit differs per day and situation?

15.1 Breaking the Limit with Drugs

Emotions can be greatly amplified or numbed by medication and drugs. Social anxieties disappear like snow in the sun when you've had alcohol. The logical part of your brain is numb. You are much less concerned with the limits you set without using alcohol. Sometimes limits have even disappeared completely.

SILENCE

It's therefore very logical that people with mental problems find the solution in alcohol or drugs. Because then those strange thoughts and feelings are not or much less present. These people also know very well that alcohol is not a true solution. In addition, alcohol is of course also physically addictive.

Ecstasy is a good example of an exceptional way to blow through your limit, which is impossible in a natural way. Not everyone has the same experience, but in general, you become extremely cheerful and happy after using ecstasy. You no longer have anxieties and everyone is your best friend. This is because ecstasy breaks your limit through the 100% barrier up to 200 or maybe even 500%. Something that of course, unless there is a medical cause (bipolar disorder for example), isn't possible. You read exactly how this works in your brain in theme four.

In fact, every drug does more or less the same thing. It creates a feeling that you normally can never feel. It breaks through natural limits or removes consciously imposed limits. It's therefore not surprising that hundreds of millions of people worldwide are more or less addicted to drugs, alcohol and antidepressants. Antidepressants actually limit emotions. Making anxiety less intense. Medication helps but is never a solution. You also often hear or read that people who are on antidepressants feel somewhat flattened. That makes sense because antidepressants are not aimed at just anxiety but to flatten all emotions. You can no longer go to 100% anxiety, but all emotions have leveled off to a maximum of 80%. Sometimes people can't find the solution without medication. It's a tool to learn to break your limits. In theme four I'll go into this in more detail plus natural alternatives.

Chapter 16: How your mind works

You may have read or heard that people with depression should never stop fighting. Don't give in to your negative thoughts. Never give up. Many people don't understand that you actually **should stop fighting**. That doesn't mean you are giving up but *surrender* to your thoughts and feelings. It may sound strange but negative thoughts, no matter how bad they are, are totally ok. You can't fight against your own thoughts, emotions or feelings. That's a fight you're always going to lose. Quitting fighting feels like giving up for many people. But it's the solution.

We live in a society where negative emotions have little room. We are totally stuck in our monetary system where spending money and working as much as possible (to make money) is the norm. There is little room for other things besides work. Most people are exhausted after a forty-hour work week and need the weekend to recover. Even a small thing can happen in your life to knock you out of balance. What if you lose your job tomorrow and won't be able to find a job in the next two years? Can you survive with your current lifestyle or do you have to sell your house and look for another place to live?

It's actually bizarre that we learn all kinds of things at school about biology but absolutely nothing about our brains and mind. How we think and how that affects our life. While this is many times more important than knowing where your heart is or what your liver is doing because they work on autopilot. Panic, anxiety, burnout and depression all originate in our mind. In the vast majority of cases, the cause is an incorrect thought pattern and incorrectly assessed situation(s). In only a few cases it's related to a medical cause.

SILENCE

So how does your mind actually work?

- If I tell you <u>not to think</u> about a pink elephant for the next few minutes, you'll probably think about it.
- If I tell you not to think about a pink elephant all day, what will you do?

You're not afraid of a pink elephant. It's just an exercise. At some point, you subconsciously let go of the thoughts that you should not think about a pink elephant. Your anxiety is nothing more than a pink elephant. Only you have made this pink elephant very important. As a result, you can't stop thinking about it for almost the entire day (because it's all so bad..). It's also possible that you only suffer from anxiety in certain situations. But even in those situations, you don't allow the pink elephant to be there.

The funny thing is that it's virtually impossible to consciously think about something all day long. You can test this very easily. When you wake up tomorrow say to yourself:

> "I'm going to think of a pink elephant every second of the day"

Or if you really want to challenge yourself:

> "I'm going to think about my anxieties or panics attacks every second of the day"

You're not going to succeed. That is impossible. Your mind will at some point wander and subconsciously start feeding you thoughts about something else. No matter how many times you try. Your brain works exactly the opposite of what you think:

- If you **want** to think about (or feel) something, it is ***impossible*** to think about it all day.

- If you **don't want** to think about (or feel) something, it is ***perfectly possible*** to think about it almost every second of the day.

That's why people can end up in depression. Because they are busy all day with how they feel and don't want to think in a negative way. But because they <u>don't</u> want to think about it or don't want to feel depressed, they are actually thinking about it!

It makes no difference to your mind whether you want to think about something or not. In both cases, you're thinking about it!

Conceptually, we humans understand the difference between yes and no. But our mind doesn't know that concept. Not or no means yes to the brain! "I don't want a panic attack" means you are sending a command to your mind. Your mind thinks:

> "Okay, a panic attack is dangerous and we must therefore prevent it. Let me give a few suggestions and when the time comes I'll throw in the flight and fight system. I'm ready!"

But what happens when you turn "don't" in "do"?

> "I don't want a panic attack" -> "I do want a panic attack"

If you deliberately want to think about something or want to feel a sensation then you <u>accept these</u> thoughts and accompanying feelings. It's impossible to get a panic attack by deliberately asking for one. It's literally impossible to get a red blushing face when asking for one. It's impossible for your anxiety to exist if you deliberately ask your anxiety to show itself.

SILENCE

When you consciously try to solve something, you ask your mind for a solution. Your mind will do everything it can to find a solution. You can't do that with anxiety. Because the root cause of anxiety is always thinking. You can't consciously not think about something. So you can't instruct your mind that you don't want to think about or feel X.

So the solution to end the anxiety program is the exact opposite of what you are doing and thinking right now. One of the techniques that will be discussed in detail later is to make your complaints and thoughts worse. I used this method to completely dissolve my social anxiety / red-blushing face within two weeks while battling with it for almost thirty years!

I was always afraid of getting a red face in social situations. Until I started doing the exact opposite:

> "I'm getting a red face again...., I hope people don't see it..."

If you turn this thought around:

> "I want my face to be as red as possible and I want everyone to see it!"

And then something amazing happened. My face didn't turn red at all. Actually, it was literally impossible to get a red face on demand. No matter how many times I tried. That's simply because once you expose yourself to the disaster scenario, you don't care anymore if the disaster scenario comes true or not. And once that happens, anxiety can't exist. Just think about the anxiety program steps:

1: **What if** I get a red face?
2: **Disaster scenario**: everybody can see my red face and will judge me!

Johan

3: **Attention**: In any social event, you give attention to your red face
4: **Resisting**: You try everything to prevent your face from getting red

When you deliberately want a red face, step 1 can't exist because the "what if" doesn't exist. Without "what if", there is no disaster scenario and without that, there is no reason to give attention and resist it. Result: no more anxiety and no more red face!

Once I realized that I never had a red face again. Simply because I now think the opposite of what I used to think. All negative thoughts and disaster scenarios regarding a red face suddenly disappeared. I simply don't think about it anymore. Because I don't care anymore if my face turns red. This new experience prevents the anxiety program from running the next time I encounter a social event.

It's just very contradictory. It is very logical to think that you can consciously solve something you don't want. But with anxiety, it works the exact opposite. The more you are busy resisting your anxiety and trying to solve it, the worse it gets. Regardless of whether it's emotions, thoughts, sensations or feelings.

So what you actually do by <u>deliberately thinking about something</u> is break through resistance. Because there can be no resistance if you deliberately want to think about something. Makes sense right?

16.1. Your brain can only add up and multiply thoughts

Your brain can only add up and multiply thoughts. You can't think thoughts away. Every time you pay attention and follow a thought, another thought comes along. Until the situation is resolved or as soon as you no longer see a need to think about it. This happens 100% unconsciously for almost everyone. You

SILENCE

won't reduce thoughts, but you simply think about something else.

People with anxiety are constantly adding up their thoughts and with severe anxiety and depression they are multiplying thoughts. More anxious thoughts will pop up. And that makes sense because your brain can only add and multiply thoughts. The only way to stop adding and multiplying thoughts is to think of something completely different. But the resistance to unwanted thoughts and feelings is so great and you want to stop thinking about your anxiety so badly that you start multiplying thoughts. Exactly the opposite of what you are trying to achieve!

Your mind is completely and 100% in your control. Even if it doesn't feel that way. When you have anxiety, you simply instruct your mind to be alert in situation X because it's dangerous. And your mind does exactly what you ask of it. It starts the anxiety program!

Imagine you are a security guard at a festival. You have been instructed that anyone with white shoes is not allowed to enter. Then you automatically pay extra attention to which shoes someone is wearing. The word "not" makes sure you pay extra attention.

If you instruct your brain that you should not be depressed or feel bad, your brain will pay extra attention to that. With all its consequences.

Stop trying to solve your anxiety, panic or depression by thinking about it.

Try to observe your anxiety in a neutral way. Then you are no longer adding and multiplying thoughts but just watching what happens without judgment. You can't reduce thoughts. You can't reverse the thoughts you had. The only things you can do to prevent adding up and multiplying unwanted thoughts and feelings are:

- Stop getting rid of your anxiety or depression (stop looking for a solution);
- Greet your thoughts and feelings;
- Challenge your thoughts and feelings;
- Examine your thoughts and feeling;
- Think about something else. But this doesn't work if you try to use this to stop thinking about the things that bother you.

Assignment: Now that you know how your brain and mind work, you can use this to challenge your anxiety. Instead of not thinking about something all day, try thinking about it all day. This works especially well if you have negative thoughts throughout the day. Instead of <u>not</u> wanting to be negative all day, try to be negative all day. In the case of a physical sensation, try to feel the sensation all day long. Observe what happens and write it down.

SILENCE

Summary Theme 2

In theme two you learned how anxiety works in your body and mind. Anxiety is managed and controlled by your amygdala. Your amygdala is triggered by thoughts, emotions, and sensations. Catastrophic thoughts and the resistance to these catastrophic thoughts keep your anxiety alive. Anxiety can only exist because you are thinking cognitively. You are thinking about what you think and feel.

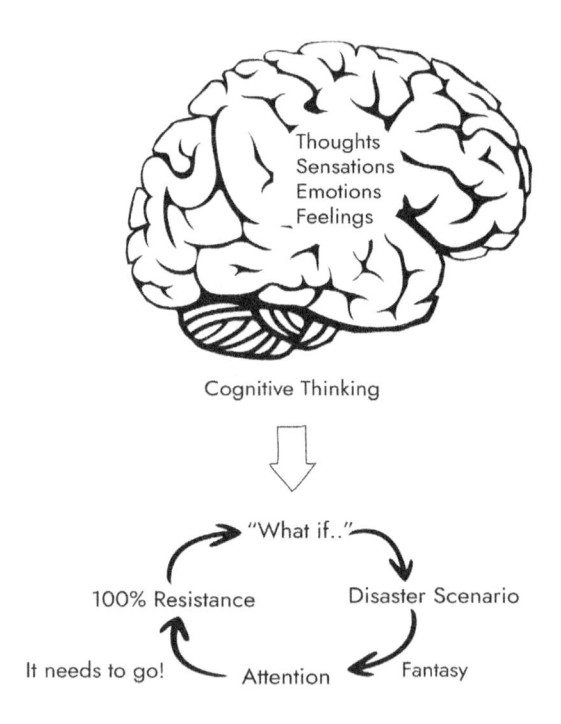

Thoughts, Sensations, Emotions, Feelings

Cognitive Thinking

⬇

"What if.." → Disaster Scenario → Fantasy → Attention → It needs to go! → 100% Resistance

You also learned that your anxiety is actually completely made up. You can't predict the future. Your anxiety has most likely never come true. Sometimes something might actually be wrong in the case of physical sensations. You can investigate this with attention exercises. If you are still in doubt after that, always check with your doctor.

Panic is 100% anxiety. The maximum anxiety that your body and mind can handle. Furthermore, the effect of anxiety and panic is the same. Thoughts, sensations or emotions always precede it. Sometimes this happens so fast that you don't feel like thinking about it and it comes completely out of nowhere. However, that is physically and mentally impossible.

Your brain works the exact opposite of what you think and want. Wanting to think about something or not is the same for the brain. In both cases, you think about it. It's impossible to consciously think about something all day long. But it is perfectly possible not wanting to think about something every second of the day. The only difference is that in the first case you accept the thoughts and seek them out. In the second case, you build up resistance and you don't want to have these thoughts or feelings. That just makes you think about it even more.

Every person with anxiety sets a limit. There are many people who try to increase or decrease their limits with drugs, alcohol or medication. This weakens your conscious thoughts and allows you to be more of what is. However, medication ensures that all your other emotions are also weakened. In addition, drugs and alcohol can cause physical addiction.

The following assignments were discussed in theme 2:

- **Assignment:** Can you convince yourself 100%?
- **Assignment:** Check with yourself whether your fantasy actually comes true.
- **Assignment:** Think about your own anxiety symptoms. What are you afraid of?

SILENCE

- **Assignment:** Now that you know how your brain works, you can use it to your advantage. Instead of not thinking about something all day, try thinking about it all day.

Theme 3: Methods to stop the anxiety program from running

In theme 3 we'll work with different techniques to accept and challenge your anxieties. All techniques are equally effective. But it may be that a certain technique works better for you than the other. So try them all out. Finally, you'll learn when your anxieties are resolved (accepted) and how to find out.

We are not actually going to stop the anxiety program from running, because that is not possible. But you can make sure that you let the anxiety program run so it stops automatically. And with these methods you can also prevent the anxiety program from running the next time you are in an anxious situation.

SILENCE

Chapter 17: At what point do you get stuck in the anxiety program?

Before we go through all the techniques, you first need to know where things are going wrong. There comes a time when "What if..." thoughts and disaster scenarios run through your mind. Maybe that's only in a certain situation or immediately when you get out of bed. This is very important to investigate because once you know where things go wrong, you also know when you can address your behavior and challenge your thoughts.

This was my personal situation:

What do I experience and when does it happen:

- **Sensation:** Heart palpitations (due to stress)
    - It usually starts when I'm in bed
- **Sensation:** Feeling of stress
    - Entire day
- **Thoughts:** This is not good, what if I get sick of stress. I can't sleep because of these heart palpitations, so much stress is not good for my body, etc.

    - Entire day
- **Feeling:**
    - Feeling of general discomfort. Not feeling well.
    - Powerless
    - frustration
    - Anxious

What if:

- What if I can't sleep because of this feeling of stress/palpitations?

Johan

- What if this isn't good for my body so much stress?
- What if I get sick (cancer etc)?
- What if I have too much stress?
- What if I can't fall asleep?

Disaster scenarios:

- Another bad night's sleep, I'll be exhausted tomorrow.
- I won't be able to sleep and I'll be tired all day
- Poor sleep is not good for my body. Something will happen.
- Poor sleep plus stress is extra bad for my health…
- I'm never getting rid of this stress…
- I don't know what to do… what should I do…

What do I give attention:

- I'm giving attention to whatever I feel in my body. These are a number of things that keep coming back:
    - Palpitations when I'm in bed and want to sleep (sometimes during the day too);
    - Focusing on a feeling of stress in my stomach during the day;
    - Feeling stressed / tense muscles in my head (I also think that there is stress in my head);
    - Weird focus on how I look through my eyes. That makes everything spin etc.

What am I doing when all of this happens:

- I'm going to focus on a technique of not feeling all of the above. A technique to get rid of the feeling.

How am I feeling:

- I'm going to focus even more on the feeling of stress, which becomes even more present. I try to stop it but I

SILENCE

can't. I'm going to scan my whole body and every little sensation is magnified. I try to push it away, I don't want to feel it, it has to go. I feel stressed.

My panic attacks mainly occurred while driving and during the night. I was afraid that the panic attack would make me lose control of the car. That I would have an accident. As soon as I got in the car my first thought was:

"What if I have a panic attack and cause an accident…"

The result was that I was scanning my body for a panic attack while driving. I know what a panic attack feels like. Once you know that, you can try to block that sensation by focusing on it. In the beginning, I had panic attacks several times a day. I was so afraid of not being able to sleep that I even had panic attacks in my bed.

So for me personally it was pretty intense. I immediately started the anxiety program as soon as I got out of bed. The first thing I did was scan with my attention to see if I was still stressed. And of course, I still had stress! Stress because I'm stressed. Anxiety about anxiety.

Assignment: Write down for yourself in detail what you think and do as soon as you are in a situation that makes you anxious. Write it down in detail. Analyze your own behavior as an outsider. You may not be able to do that at the moment. But try your best. Write down in detail what you are thinking and what you are doing at that moment. Take my personal experiences as an example. If you're not sure, stop reading for now and take a few days to write down your thoughts and behavior.

Once you've written this down, that's the basis you can work with. You now know what kind of behavior you show during anxious situations and what thoughts go with it. In the following

Johan

chapters, we will go through several techniques that will try to unlearn your behavior and think differently.

Chapter 18: Other Root Causes

In the previous themes, you learned a lot about anxiety, how your brain works and where exactly things go wrong in your case. It's also possible that other emotions are in your way.

It's impossible to conclude that anxiety can always be solved by doing X. Each person is too unique for that. The techniques in this book are suitable for accepting the vast majority of anxieties. But sometimes the anxiety has to do with something completely different. It may well be that there is an underlying emotion that prevents you from feeling anxiety. Then it's not the anxiety that is the problem, but the underlying emotion.

You may be sad and angry because you think you're a failure. And that's why you've become anxious to do new things. The anxiety then arises from your sadness, anger and uncertainty. You can't accept anxiety if you don't first accept your sadness, anger, and insecurity.

For me personally, there was a lot of frustration and anger involved. I'm someone with iron discipline. I will continue until it's resolved. But anxiety can't be solved. Anger and frustration often prevailed. My expectations were totally wrong because I didn't know how anxiety works. In addition, I am also someone who likes control. Of course, control and anxiety don't go hand in hand. Anxiety (and any other emotion) can't be controlled.

Of course, I don't know your personal situation. So I can't say whether it's really anxiety that's bothering you or whether there's something more behind it. Often you need guidance with underlying complaints to see if there is something more behind it. Therapy can help with this. However, a specific anxiety therapy only focuses on anxiety. If the techniques in the next

Johan

chapter don't really help you, try using the same techniques but targeting the other emotions that are bothering you.

Chapter 19: Different Techniques (Remember your Intention and your Goal)

We're not trying to get rid of your negative thoughts or feelings. These techniques are all very effective. But they don't always work right away. You have to practice as much as you can.

Accept that you won't get rid of your anxiety within a week or month. This way you ensure that you don't create high expectations. I know all too well that you would like to get rid of your anxiety. Preferably yesterday. But it doesn't work like that. It can be a long process. But have faith and patience.

Always remember your personal goal that you wrote down. It can never be the goal to get rid of your anxiety. That it has to go. If that's still your goal, the techniques are of no use. Before you start applying the techniques, it's very important that you make time and space to practice. Even if you don't feel like it. I remember very well that I never felt like doing an exercise. I went through it quickly and didn't make time for it. And then afterwards I was complaining that it didn't work and I got frustrated. Take your time!

19.1. Intention

Without the right intention, you simply can't accept anxiety and all techniques in this book have zero effect. But this is also the hardest part of all. And there is no guidance for this. I can't tell you how to do this. Because it can't be explained in words. It comes down to really believing what you are telling yourself. You can't fool yourself. You can't tell yourself

Johan

> "I really want to get a panic attack right now!"

While in the meantime you don't want a panic attack at all. Does that make sense?

A personal example:

I was very bothered by physical sensations that I didn't want to feel. A body scan worked very well for me. Because with the body scan, I went looking for these sensations instead of wishing them away. At one point I was stressed all day. In the evening I performed a body scan and I was completely relaxed. My mind wandered and I almost fell asleep. So the body scan worked very well! I was no longer stressed and my thoughts about the stress were gone. Simply because I didn't think about the stress but was scanning my whole body with a positive mindset.

The next day I was very stressed again. I didn't know what to do. Then I suddenly remembered that I had done a body scan the previous day and that it worked very well. So I immediately thought this was the solution. Only this time I was going to do the body scan with the <u>intention/expectation that the stress would decrease</u>. Do you think that helped? No, not at all! My intention and purpose of doing the exercise were totally wrong.

In short:

- During the first body scan my intention was to do a body scan without expectations
- During the second body scan, my intention was to make my feeling of stress disappear.

I did the exact same exercise. The first time it had the desired result, the second time it didn't work at all. The only difference was my intention. It's therefore extremely important that you mean what you say to yourself. That's why it's very important that your goal / intention is very clear. This goal and intention can't have anything related to getting rid of your negative thoughts or feelings or feeling good again. As you learned, that is the root cause of your problems!

19.3. Different techniques to deal with your anxiety and panic

It is best to try a technique every day for at least a month. Write down the results for each day. Write down what you feel and what you think. This can be done during or after performing the technique. Maybe the first technique works very well for you and you don't even need the other techniques. There is no fixed step-by-step plan, you have to work this out yourself because every person is different. Simply start with technique 1 and try it out for a month. You can also combine techniques. And once you understand how anxiety works and go through different techniques, you already know how to create your own techniques.

Disclaimer: Only perform all techniques in a safe environment. If you have serious complaints or suicidal thoughts, always contact a professional.

Technique 1: Greet your anxiety

All anxiety wants is to get your attention. Anxiety wants to be heard. And that only happens when **you** start the conversation. Your anxiety is constantly trying to greet you, but you ignore the signals. A good conversation always starts with a greeting.

Welcome anxiety. Greet your anxiety!

- "Welcome anxiety/feeling, nice to have you back"
- "What can I do for you?"
- "Good morning anxiety!"

Johan

Thoughts
Sensations
Emotions
Feelings

"What if.."
100% Resistance   Disaster Scenario
It needs to go!   Attention

Good morning, anxiety.
How are you?

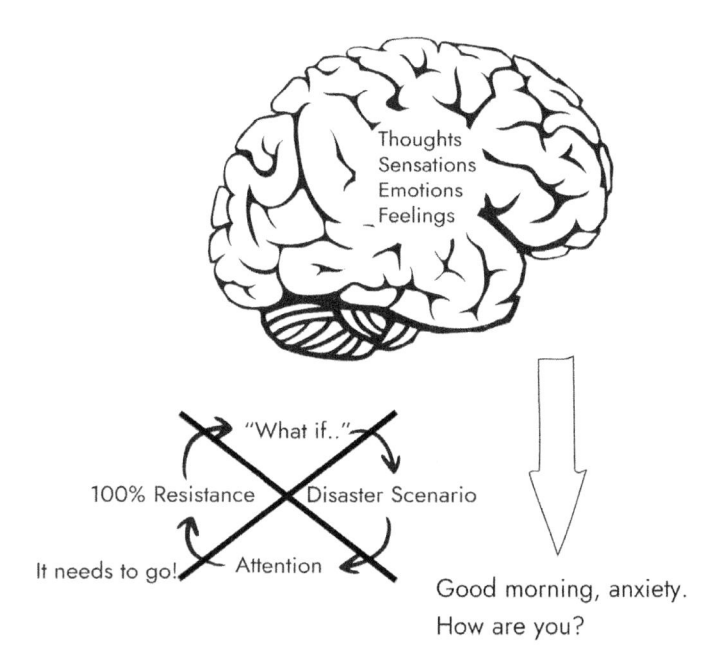

Greeting your anxiety prevents you from getting caught up in "what if" thoughts and disaster scenarios. Greeting your anxiety is the first step in starting a conversation. You don't have to become friends right away. But every friendship begins with a greeting. When you visit your best friend, you always greet each other and ask how things are going. The ultimate goal is to see your anxiety as a good friend.

Although this can be used as a separate technique, I would strongly advise to always use this technique first and then combine it with other techniques. Always greet your anxiety before you do anything else.

Assignment for this technique:

First you have to **a**cknowledge your anxiety. That might be a feeling, sensation or just thoughts. The second step is to

SILENCE

connect with that feeling, sensation or thought. The third and last step is greeting the feeling, sensation or thought.

1. Acknowledge your anxiety by saying "I feel stressed right now" or "I'm having anxious thoughts right now"
2. Connect with these feelings or thoughts. Try to be with them instead of not wanting them.
3. Greet your feelings or thoughts. Welcome them.

You can remember the steps as ACG. Acknowledge, Connect, Greet. Take a few minutes and practice this right now. If you're not feeling anxious right now, try thinking of something you don't want to think about and follow the above steps.

When to perform this technique:

With all the techniques described in this book, it's super important that you also apply them when you're not anxious!

Many people think they don't have to do anything if they're not feeling anxious for a while. But that's a very good moment to greet your anxiety. So you can do this technique as often as you want. It doesn't matter if it's thoughts, feelings or sensations. Try to greet them at fixed times:

- When you get out of bed;
- When you go to sleep;
- In situations where you're anxious.

Variation 1: Look at your anxiety from its point of view

Everything you read or hear about anxiety is always from the point of view of the person experiencing the anxiety. Have you ever thought about what your anxiety feels? Do you think your anxiety likes the fact that you are pushing it away every time it tries to contact you? Your anxiety only wants to greet you, but you slam the door in its face without saying "hi". Your anxiety feels completely misunderstood and tries to get your attention in all kinds of ways. How would you feel if someone you'd like to connect with flatly ignored you completely?

It may sound strange to think of anxiety as something that has feelings. But your body has feelings that go beyond the mind. Anxiety wants to go somewhere. But if it has nowhere to go, it will accumulate in your body. A tense feeling in your stomach, a tight throat, hunched shoulders, pain in the lower back, a burning sensation in your throat. How do you think your anxiety feels about you?

Assignment for this technique:

Visualize your anxiety from its point of view. Give attention to the place in your body where your anxiety is most expressed (including thoughts). Maybe the anxiety can tell you how it feels.

Technique 2: Challenge your anxieties

By challenging your anxieties, you're doing the exact opposite of what you are doing right now. Right now you want to get rid of anxiety. You don't want to think about it. But as you know by now and experience yourself, this doesn't help. It only makes the anxiety worse. But by doing the exact opposite you'll see that your anxiety has all the space it needs. All your anxiety wants is to be heard.

What happens when you start challenging anxiety? Then you ***accept*** the thoughts and feelings that are released. Simply because you are deliberately wanting to feel anxiety. You can't resist something you deliberately want to happen.

I quickly accepted one of my social anxieties this way. I had anxiety about blushing (red face) all my life. In group

SILENCE

conversations, presentations, meetings, at the checkout in a supermarket, you name it. I suffered from this in literally every social situation for over twenty-five years.
I avoided these situations as much as possible:

- During other people's presentations, I would sit out of their line of sight so they couldn't see me or ask me questions;
- At the checkout in the supermarket, I always went to a self-service point where you can pay for groceries yourself to avoid social interaction with the cashier;
- Have someone else present as much as possible;
- Don't stand out too much in groups;
- Keeping quiet in discussions while I did have an opinion;
- Etc.

But this avoidance behavior solves nothing. Because the next time I had to give a presentation, my anxieties immediately surfaced again. And this time I couldn't hide behind somebody else. How did I get rid of this anxiety after suffering for twenty-five years? Actually, it was quite simple for me. All my life I always had the same catastrophic thoughts while giving a presentation or in other social situations:

- "I don't want a red face.."
- "Someone will notice that I turn red…"
- "Ooh, I can feel my face turning red again, stop!"
- "What will other people think of my red face…."

Time and time again I had the same or a variant of the above thoughts. With a focus on my red face. I always squinted at my nose to see how red my face was... Then I started to challenge these thoughts and the feeling of a red face. By thinking the exact opposite. I changed the words "not" and "don't" to "I do want" and "bring it on!".

"I want to have a red face right now!"

Johan

My face no longer turned red. Because I said to myself "I want to have a red face right now" the anxiety finally felt accepted. It finally got permission to be there. When I first started practicing this it was like a switch flipped in my brain. My thoughts were:

    "Ahh, that's how it works!"

and

    "I'm sure I'll never get a red face again!"

SILENCE

Thoughts
Sensations
Emotions
Feelings

"What if.."

~~100% Resistance~~   Disaster Scenario

~~It needs to go!   Attention~~

Bring it on!

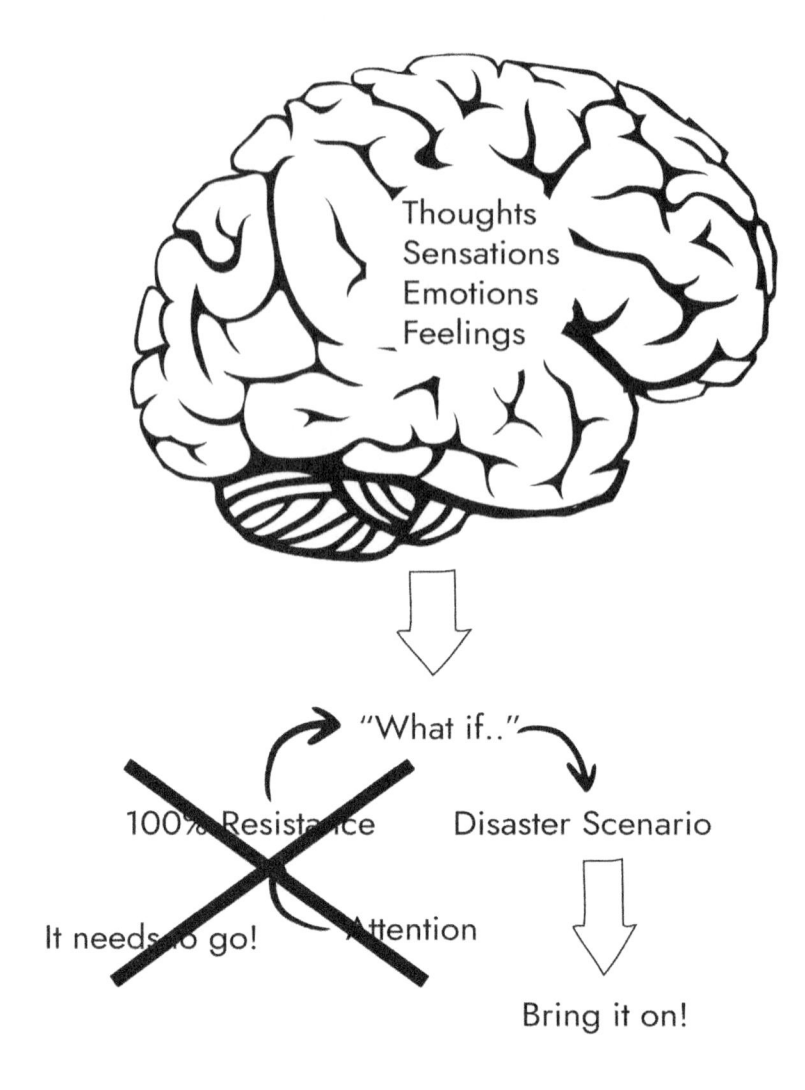

These positive thoughts were very powerful. I firmly believed that this was the solution. And so it was. All I've done is challenge my red face to turn red. Some other examples:

- "I'm going to have a panic attack soon..." -> "I want a panic attack right now"
- "My heartbeat is way too fast" -> "I want my heart to beat faster!"

- "I feel dizzy" -> "I want to get dizzy right now"
- "I don't want to blush" -> "I want to blush right now!"

These examples mainly deal with sensations but work just as well with thoughts:

- "I don't want to think about this.." -> "I do want to think about this right now"
- "Stop all those thoughts!" -> "Bring on all those thoughts!"
- "I can't fall asleep now…" -> "I don't want to sleep"
- "I'm afraid of causing an accident" -> "I want to cause an accident right now!"

On the last thought, of course, it's not the intention to overturn the wheel of your car while driving. But a way to challenge your thoughts about causing an accident.

You can apply this technique in several ways. You can challenge your thoughts, but sometimes it's also necessary to challenge your feelings. In the case of my social anxiety, I didn't just tell myself I wanted to get a red face. I also tried to evoke the red feeling in my face by focusing on it.

Assignment for this technique:

The next time your anxieties bother you, challenge them. These can be thoughts, sensations or other emotions. If you're afraid of fainting in a supermarket, try the technique at home first. Go to your bedroom and sit on the edge of your bed. Take a few deep breaths. Say to yourself:

> "I want to pass out NOW"

Make sure your intention is real. Try to faint by just thinking about it. That you should pass out right now. Bring it on! Observe what happens.

SILENCE

Hold on to this mindset and the associated feeling. As soon as you're ready, you go to the supermarket. Not to buy food but to pass out. As you get closer and closer to the supermarket, your mind will try to drive you crazy. That you're about to faint and you need to get out of here. You start multiplying thoughts. Repeat to these thoughts that you don't mind fainting, but want to faint. In many cases of fainting, it's not so much about the fainting itself but about what other people will think if you pass out in a crowd. Then tell yourself that you don't care what other people think if you pass out in front of them.

Do you suffer from social anxiety? Then there are often sensations such as sweating, turning red, trembling voice, and strange feelings in your head and stomach. Challenge all these feelings. I want to turn red now. I want to get sweaty hands now. I will now try to vibrate as much as possible with my voice. Go with your attention to what you don't want and challenge it.

Variation 1: Make your anxiety worse

A variation of this technique is making your anxiety much worse. You read that right. Find the absolute worst possible outcome of your anxiety. If you're afraid of getting a red face, tell yourself:

- "I want to get as red as possible now"
- "I want to get extremely red right now!"
- "I hope everyone sees how red I am!"
- "This is not enough…! Come on! Give me everything you've got!"

Challenging your anxieties and making them worse will take you even further toward your anxieties. You get to the core of your anxiety. Just stand in front of a mirror and try to get a red face on command. Whether you have the anxiety of blushing or not, it's impossible to blush on command. No matter how bad your

Johan

social anxiety is. It's also impossible to blush on command when facing 200 people during a presentation.

If you're afraid of a panic attack, try to consciously evoke it. Sit in a safe and quiet place. Make yourself comfortable and tell yourself that you want to have the worst panic attack right now. As you do so, focus your attention on the sensations you normally feel during a panic attack. Make it the worst panic attack you ever had.

The trick is to do the same when you are in a situation where you would normally get a panic attack. And of course, it might not work the first few times and you'll still have a panic attack. That's OK!. This has everything to do with your intention. If you truly 100% want a panic attack right now, it will never happen. It takes practice so take your time.

SILENCE

Thoughts
Sensations
Emotions
Feelings

⬇

"What if.."

~~100% Resistance~~   Disaster Scenario

~~It needs to go!~~   ~~Attention~~

Bring it on!

⬇

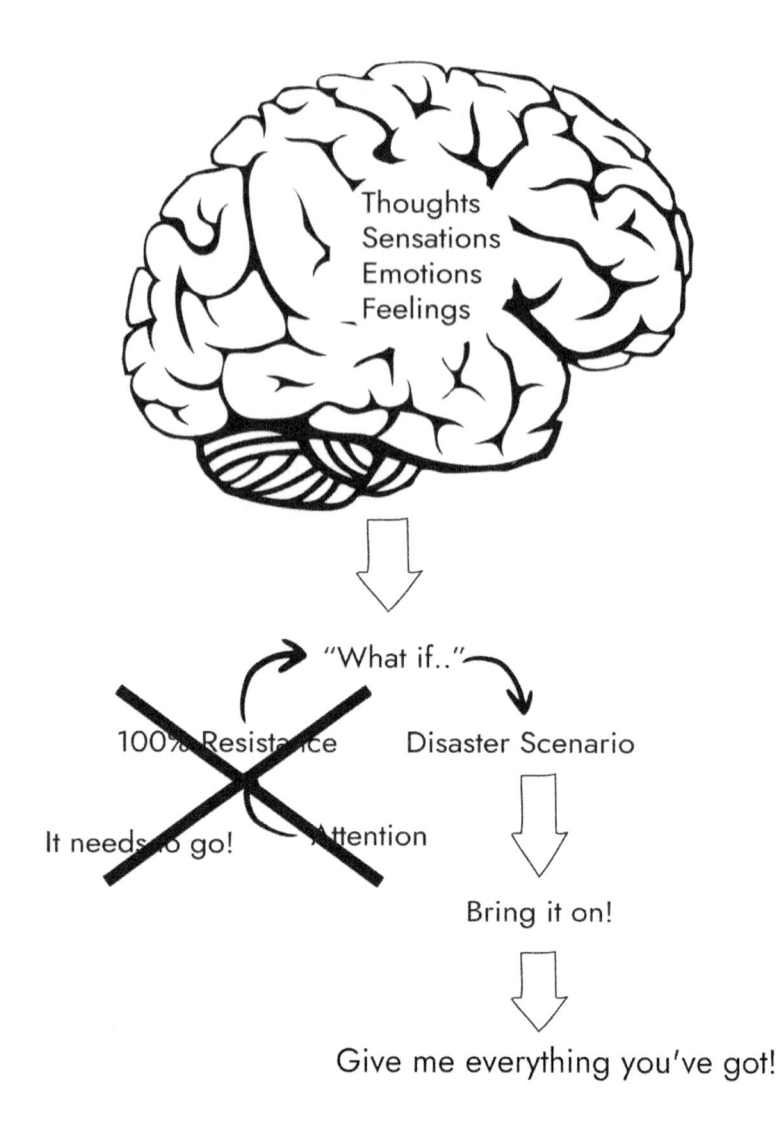

Give me everything you've got!

When to use this technique:

Every time your anxieties arise. But also schedule moments during the day to consciously evoke your anxiety. Even if it doesn't bother you at all at that moment.

Johan

What anxiety can you use this technique for:

This technique works very well with physical sensations. Think of social situations (blushing) and hypochondria. This technique also works very well for panic attacks. Instead of avoiding the sensations, you make them worse. Realize that it's **impossible** to make your anxiety symptoms worse if you really mean it. The more you try to make your anxiety worse, the **fewer** complaints you will eventually have.

Technique 3: Debunk your catastrophic thoughts

This is a very powerful technique. With this technique, you'll look for evidence to debunk your catastrophic thoughts. As you know by now, your catastrophic thoughts are 99.9% just fantasy. You make predictions about the future or the past. But you can't see into the future or change the past so you don't know what's going to happen at all.

This is also a tricky technique so use it wisely. The reason I'm mentioning this is because anxiety can't exist when you don't think about it. With this exercise you're going to think about it. Please keep that in mind. This technique is only used to figure out what you are thinking is actually true. And once you figured out it's not true you stop thinking about it.

If you're afraid that there is something wrong with your heart, you'll focus on your heart. As a result, you'll feel all the sensations in detail. And you can even conjure up sensations that aren't actually there. So something is definitely happening because you feel something. Only the catastrophic thoughts that follow are wrong. For example, you can think:

> "I'll have a heart attack any time soon!"

SILENCE

At that moment you can apply this technique to challenge and negate the catastrophic thought:

- "Am I really having a heart attack?"
- "I've had these symptoms a thousand times but I've never had a heart attack"
- "According to the doctor, my heart is fine, so what makes it different this time?"
- "Is it really my heart what I feel right now?"
- "What evidence do I have that there is something wrong with my heart?"

Then there are people who think "yes, but... I've read or heard somewhere that someone who was 100% healthy just had a heart attack!"

You don't know whether that story is true. Often people don't eat and live as healthy as they appear. Because healthy eating and living is a profession in itself. There are many myths about healthy and unhealthy foods. And you don't just get a heart attack. Just because they can't find the cause doesn't mean this person was 100% healthy. In fact, literally every human being on this planet can have a heart attack out of nowhere. Chances are small, but not inevitable.

You're more likely to win the lottery than to just have a heart attack. If you pay close attention to your diet and exercise at least a few times a week, the risk of a heart attack is negligible. You don't need scientific studies for that.

With this technique, it's important to collect as much evidence as possible. Look for reliable sources that confirm your "What if..." thoughts and disaster scenarios. With your research, you should be able to convince yourself and someone else with real evidence that your "what if" thoughts and disaster scenarios are correct and 100% true.

Johan

Thoughts
Sensations
Emotions
Feelings

→ "What if.."

100% Resistance   Disaster Scenario

It needs to go!   Attention

Is this really true? What evidence do I have?

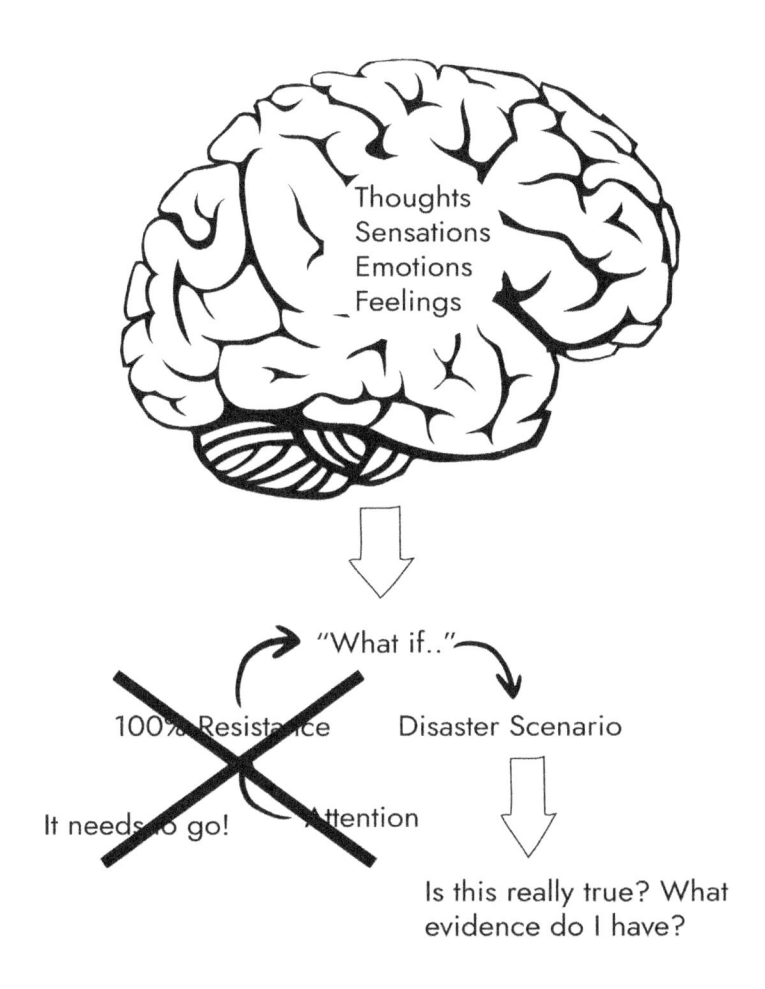

This is pretty powerful for thoughts like:

"I'll never get rid of this…"

I had these thoughts many times and I still got rid of my complaints. THe above thought simply not true because you can't know what will happen in the future.

Assignment:

Conduct a large-scale survey about your anxious thoughts. Find proof that your thoughts and disaster scenarios are correct and 100% true. Is it really true what you think? Or what you think will happen? Do you have proof for that? And can you convince your best friend with this proof and will he/she agree 100%?

But be aware you are now discussing your own thoughts. Don't get into a discussion with your own thoughts. Observe them, write them down and figure out if they are true.

Use this technique for:

All types of anxiety. The next time you can stop your catastrophic thought by saying to yourself:

> "That's nice and all what you're telling me, but I've already researched that and it's simply not correct."

Tip: Combine this technique with technique 2 (make things worse). You first check whether it's really true what you think. Then turn it all the way around by thinking:

- "According to my research I'm not having a heart attack. It's probably a twitched muscle."
- "Okay, let's see. Bring on a heart attack!"
- "I want a heart attack right now!"

Technique 4: Explosion of negative thoughts and feelings

What you're going to do with this technique is simply to tell your mind to be as negative as possible. Command your mind to think extremely negatively. Make it as absurd as possible. Think of as many disaster scenarios as possible. Try to evoke an explosion of negative thoughts, feelings and emotions.

Johan

The underlying idea is that people often only want to think positively:

- "I don't want these negative thoughts"
- "I just want to think positive…"
- "I don't want to think about that…"
- "I don't want to feel depressed.."

As you know by now, your brain works exactly the other way around. Whatever thoughts you try to ignore will add up or get multiplied. So whether you want to think about something or not, for the mind it's all the same. Negative thinking is allowed! And especially if you're generally a negative thinker. Try being even more negative than you already are.

SILENCE

Thoughts
Sensations
Emotions
Feelings

⬇

"What if.."

~~100% Resistance~~   Disaster Scenario

~~It needs to go!~~   ~~Attention~~

⬇

Try to be as negative as possible.

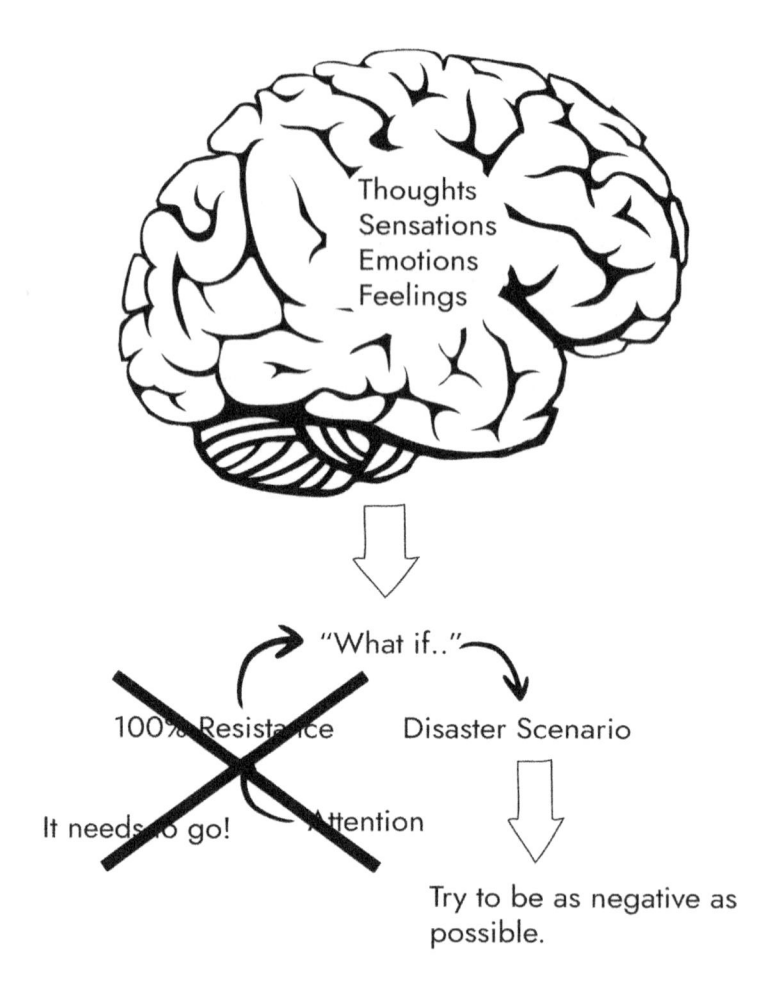

You can think whatever you want during this assignment. It doesn't matter anymore. Make it as negative as possible.

Assignment:

Plan a moment in your day, a few times a week, for about 15 - 30 min. During this time, the only goal is to be as negative as possible. Focus on your anxiety. Or maybe something else that's bothering you. Just consciously think negatively. Let your mind come up with as many negative scenarios as possible and observe what happens.

What anxiety can you use this technique for:

This technique works very well if you have continuous negative thoughts. Like your head is about to explode. You think you're going crazy. And you want it to stop. If you experience moments like this, apply this technique. Instead of trying to control your continuous flow of negative thoughts, you allow all negative thoughts. Try to consciously add up more negative thoughts. Try to be as negative as possible. Your continuous stream of thoughts arises because you don't want negative thoughts. The continuous stream of negative thoughts are only there because you are fighting them. It doesn't stop when you want it to stop. But you'll notice that you'll get fewer negative thoughts once you challenge your mind to generate more negative thoughts.

Technique 5: Surrender to your emotion(s)

By surrendering to your emotions you give them full space. Surrendering is different from giving up. This technique consists of two parts with a guided video on youtube:

- Accept the emotion
- Surrender to the emotion

Choose a quiet place and sit or lie down. The first step is to accept the emotion. If you're anxious, tell yourself it's totally "ok" to be anxious. It is totally "ok" to feel emotions. Identify that you are now anxious (or another emotion):

- "I am anxious right now"

SILENCE

Become very aware of the emotion you are feeling right now. In addition to anxiety, this can also be another emotion such as anger or frustration. Identify what emotion you are feeling right now. Take time to feel the emotion.

The next step is complete surrender to the emotion. Make yourself vulnerable. It's totally "ok" to be anxious. Take 15 minutes and sit in your emotion. Go to your emotion and feel it:

- "I feel anxious right now"
- "It's totally okay to be anxious"
- Feel the anxiety

Important with this technique is that you really have to feel the anxiety as an emotion and not purely with your thoughts. You can say in your mind that it is "ok" to be anxious, but if you are still making up all kinds of catastrophic thoughts in the meantime, you are still in your head and not in the emotion. Don't jump into the pool, but sit on the edge with your feet in the water. Try to take some distance.

You basically need to stop having the feeling that whatever you don't want needs to go.

You can distance yourself by no longer being interested in the thoughts that come to your mind. You don't ignore your thoughts but you don't follow them. Also thoughts like "Am I doing this right?" or "This doesn't work" you can let go. Just stop paying attention.

Assignment:

Do this exercise every day for 30 minutes. If you need less time, that's fine too. Try not to be in your head but look in the emotion you are targeting. A guided video you can use: https://youtu.be/pzKZSYq0uvs

Johan

What anxiety can you use this technique for:

This technique is mainly aimed at emotions in general. Such as sadness, anger or frustration. You can only accept anxiety if you accept all other emotions as well. Anxiety is often accompanied by anger and frustration. Why me? Why doesn't it work? I'm never getting out of here. Why do I feel this way…?

Technique 6: Accept the outcome of your disaster

People live their lives based on self-invented rules and laws and always try to adhere to them. That almost never works in practice and what follows is resistance. Negative emotions are not allowed (including anxiety, anger and sadness). Everyone wants to feel good and be happy all the time.

It's "OK" how you feel. Even if you feel shit all day. Or maybe the whole week or the whole month. Even if you think you're a failure. As soon as you start resisting how you feel, you'll only feel worse.

If you're "OK" with the things that might happen, you are no longer afraid of the anxiety (anxiety of the anxiety). Your anxiety is not gone, but you are no longer afraid of the outcome. Naturally, your brain will immediately scream that you are in danger. That you must flee and run for your life. With this technique, you tell that voice in your head that you don't care. That you don't care anymore what happens or could possibly happen. Just let it happen.

SILENCE

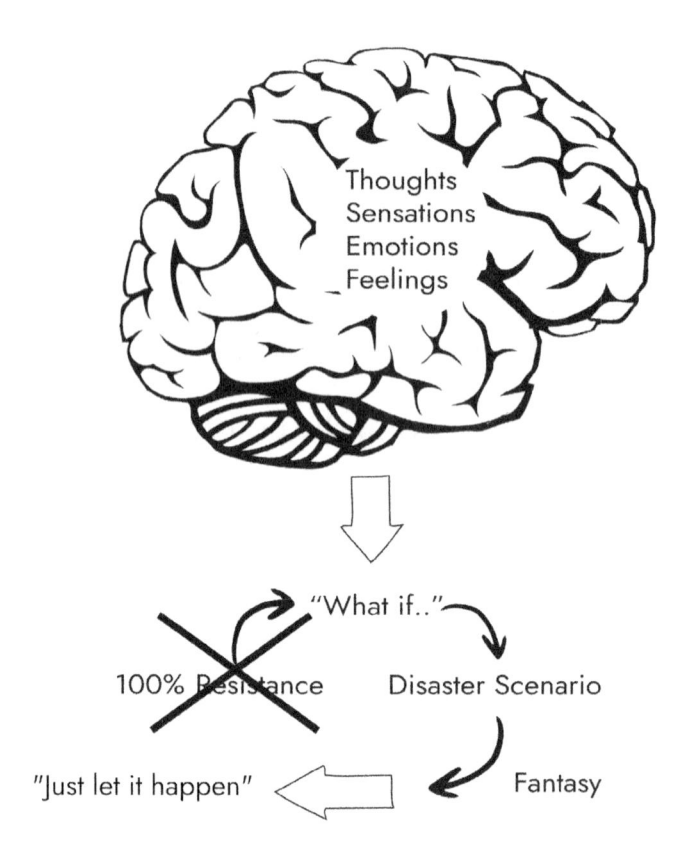

In the example of fainting in the supermarket, it's not so much about the fainting itself. But what other people will think. There are many people in a supermarket. And there is a good chance that there are people who know you. Wouldn't it be terrible if these people saw you pass out in the supermarket? If you no longer care what other people think about you, then you're no longer afraid of fainting. Just let it happen.

It's not the circumstances that make us uncomfortable or suffer, but how we think about it. Whatever your disaster scenario is, just let it all happen and see what actually happens.

Assignment for this technique:

Johan

The next time your anxiety starts to bother you again, tell yourself:

> "I don't care what happens. Do what you want, I allow it to happen"

Technique 7: The cloud technique

This technique works very well for falling asleep. Many people who deal with anxiety every day have trouble falling asleep. You fall asleep when you stop thinking. But you can't consciously stop thinking by thinking you want to stop thinking. That's simply not possible. This is an automatic process. You'll stop thinking once your mind drifts off. And that can only happen when you are so tired you can't think anymore or when you let go of all the stuff that is bothering you.

The technique works as follows:

You can't prevent a thought from entering your mind, but you can decide not to follow it. You visualize that every thought that comes into your mind will turn into a cloud. And this cloud then falls apart and vanishes. You apply this to the first words of every sentence that comes to your mind.

A few examples:

When you start worrying, it will look something like this:

- "I would like to sleep now…"
- "I can still feel my heart beating…"
- "I can't sleep…"
- "I only have 7 hours left to sleep. I really need to fall asleep…"
- "Today was another bad day…"

SILENCE

- "I really need to do something about situation x at work"
- "I hope I can make it till the end of the month, I really need some money!"
- Etc.

This list is endless and will be different for everyone. It doesn't matter what you think about either. With the cloud technique, you'll neutralize these thoughts into a cloud. But you're going to do this before you can finish the sentence:

- "I do..."
- "I feel my..."
- "I..."
- "I still have ..."
- "Today..."
- "I..."

You will very consciously cut off every beginning of a sentence and turn it into a cloud. A cloud that then disappears into nothingness. As if the cloud dissolves itself in a millisecond. Letting the thought go before you can finish the sentence in your head.

Because you're very focused on cutting off the sentence and trying to turn it into a cloud, you can't end up in "what if" thoughts or disaster scenarios. You can turn it into a game. By telling your brain:

"Bring on all the negative thoughts you have"

Then try to make a cloud out of them. This is extra powerful because if you allow your brain to deliberately create negative worrying thoughts, you'll notice that you have a hard time conjuring negative thoughts.

Assignment:

Johan

Use this technique every night before going to sleep if you have trouble falling asleep. Try to cut your sentences off at the first word of the sentence and visualize the thought dissolving like a cloud into nothingness.

Variation 1: Make your thoughts extremely slow

Often when you start worrying, the speed at which thoughts follow is very fast. One thought after another pops up. However, you can decide how quickly and how often these thoughts come in. You can determine the speed of the voice in your head.

- Consciously take deeper breaths;
- You're only allowed to think one word during each breath.

For example,

> "I had a very bad day, this and that happened etc."

- Breath in for a few seconds, once you breathe out you say the word "I"
- Breath in for a few seconds, once you breathe out you say the word "had"
- Breath in for a few seconds, once you breathe out you say the word "a"
- Breath in for a few seconds, once you breathe out you say the word "very"
- Breath in for a few seconds, once you breathe out you say the word "bad"
- Breath in for a few seconds, once you breathe out you say the word "day"

You'll notice that there are way fewer thoughts coming in. You can apply this technique any time you notice your inner voice is too fast and want to slow down.

Technique 8: You win

Anxiety, panic, but also depression are always related to a struggle. A battle against thoughts, against the future or the past. It's a battle with yourself. But the outcome of the fight is already decided before you even begin. <u>You're not going to win the fight</u>. You're fighting against your mind. If you win, you've beaten your own mind. That doesn't really sound logical, does it?

You sometimes read that people who are in depression should not give in to their thoughts. Don't give up fighting the demons. But fighting and not wanting to give up is the <u>root cause of depression</u>. There is, of course, a whole process that precedes this. No one just ends up in a depression overnight. Somewhere during this process, more and more resistance is built up.

Many people see anxiety, panic and depression as a demon that must be conquered and destroyed. Then a fight begins between you and your demons. But with this technique, instead of fighting you let your demons win. Take your loss. Give your demons/feelings/thoughts a name or form and very consciously say:

> "Okay, you win. I surrender.. Do whatever you want"

Let your demons win the battle. Because what actually happens when you give up the fight? What happens when you let your demons win? What happens when your demons keep yelling that you're worthless and you say, "ok you win, I'm worthless"?

All your demons want is confirmation that they are being heard. Then they leave you alone. It's just that people are so fixated on defeating their demons while the solution lies on the other side. Trying to defeat them is the root cause.

Johan

Surrender to your anxiety. Give your anxiety the win. You don't have to win every game. Take your loss. Surrender. Give your anxiety all the freedom and let it do what it wants. You're not a weakling if you surrender. If you were to step into the ring with the kickboxing world champion (Rico Verhoeven), you also know in advance that you're going to lose. So you better not step into the ring at all. Then it is a very smart decision not to fight and to surrender.

Raise the white flag. Surrender to your thoughts, sensations and emotions. I have personally applied this to my stress complaints. At one point I was fighting the stress so hard that I thought:

> "You know what, you win. You (the stress) may take over my whole body. Send all the stress to every nook and cranny in my body. I give up. You win…"

What happened? I collapsed like a house of cards. I had built up so much tension. My muscles were completely stiff with tension. When I surrendered, the tension was gone and I realized how stressed I was. Not only the stress disappeared, but my mind was also completely empty. All positive and neutral thoughts poured in. Because I had finally made room and surrendered to the stress. I stopped fighting and surrendered.

Assignment for this technique:

Surrender to your anxiety. Let your anxiety win. Throw in the towel. Realize that you've lost and accept your loss. Let your thoughts, sensations and emotions take over. Let them go, let them do what they want. Observe what happens. Realize that you are not a weakling who gives up, but that you are consciously making a smart choice by surrendering.

Technique 9: Be curious about your resistance

You can't have anxiety if you don't resist the outcome. If none of the previous techniques work well for you, it's time to take a closer look at your resistance. Be curious about your resistance.

For me, looking for the ultimate technique was my resistance. No matter what exercise I did, they all stopped working. That was because I didn't have the right intention. My intention of every exercise was that my feeling of stress must go away. What actually happened is that continuously trying to do an exercise was my resistance. All the techniques in this book won't work if you think they will solve the problem. In fact, you only build up more resistance. And after reading this book you'll look for another way to get rid of it by reading another book or trying something else like therapy.

If you're constantly trying to apply techniques all day long to not feel your anxiety, try looking at it from a different angle. Resistance consists of three parts:

1. You feel a feeling, thought, sensation or emotion;
2. You start thinking about it;
3. You use a way (technique) to resist step 1.

Every time I felt my anxiety I tried to solve it with a technique. But that just caused more resistance. In my case, it worked very well to consciously look at my resistance every day. Instead of continuously trying to do an exercise, I started observing what I was actually doing. For example, I stopped applying a technique as soon as I felt anxiety coming up. I said to myself:

> "No, I'm not going to do any exercise now to get rid of the anxiety. I am now going to feel what I feel and not resist anymore"

Johan

I started observing what my resistance actually is. I started to look at it out of curiosity.

Assignment for this technique:

Be curious about your resistance. What exactly are you doing when you're resisting? Observe your behavior throughout the day. Write down the moment as soon as you start resisting. Then consciously look curiously at what solution you come up with. Instead of immediately using a technique to get rid of your anxiety, you start observing.

> "Oh yes, I'm going to resist now. I'm now trying another technique to get rid of the feeling. Let me see what techniques my brain comes up with…"

Technique 10: do nothing

The "funny" thing about anxiety is that you don't actually have to do anything about it. So far we have talked about techniques and how you can stop the anxiety program by taking action. But in the end, fully accepting your anxiety means that you <u>don't do anything about it</u>.

What do you do when you have no anxiety?

- Are you trying to get rid of it?
- Do you curse it?
- Does it have to go?
- Are you thinking about it?
- Are you involved in any way?

The answer is always no. So if you simply don't do anything, you won't be bothered by your anxieties! As soon as you give up the fight (by doing nothing) anxiety will feel heard.

SILENCE

If you're completely stuck in a web of techniques and everything, just do nothing with your thoughts and feelings for a month. No more techniques to get rid of it. No breathing exercises. No meditation. Just nothing at all. This works especially well if you have been trying many techniques, therapy and so on for a long time. <u>Just stop trying to solve the problem.</u>

I remember well that at one point a psychologist said to me:

> "This isn't working for you. Let's just stop everything for a while and then next time we'll see how we can handle this."

A weight was immediately lifted off my shoulders. Finally doing nothing at all. I was immediately a lot more relaxed. My anxiety wasn't gone. But I no longer felt the pressure to continuously plan and perform exercises.

Assignment for this technique:

For the next few weeks you'll do absolutely nothing with your anxiety. When thoughts arise, try to let them go but don't apply any techniques. Don't try to push them away, don't try to avoid situations and don't apply any techniques you learned. Acknowledge that your thoughts are there but try not to spend time on them. Only greet them and go on with your day. Try looking at it from a third person. Don't sit in your thoughts but look at it from a distance.
Summary techniques

We've discussed ten different techniques and different variations. One technique works very well in situation x and the other in situation y. Not every technique works equally well for everyone. Or maybe not at all. That's okay. Maybe a combination of all techniques works best for you.

Johan

There's no fixed step-by-step plan for your particular anxiety. But the solution is always the same: go towards it. Greet it. Challenge it. I have supplemented the techniques as I have used them. But of course, you can also give it your twist. With the thoughts that work best for you. You can basically come up with your own techniques. As long as you use it to go towards your feelings.

No person is equal. Everyone is looking for a way to deal with emotions and feelings. The only way to do that is to accept what is. There is no other way. The more you let it be what is, the less miserable you feel about it. And remember that accepting means you <u>stop</u> doing something. And in this case that is stop trying to get rid of your anxiety.

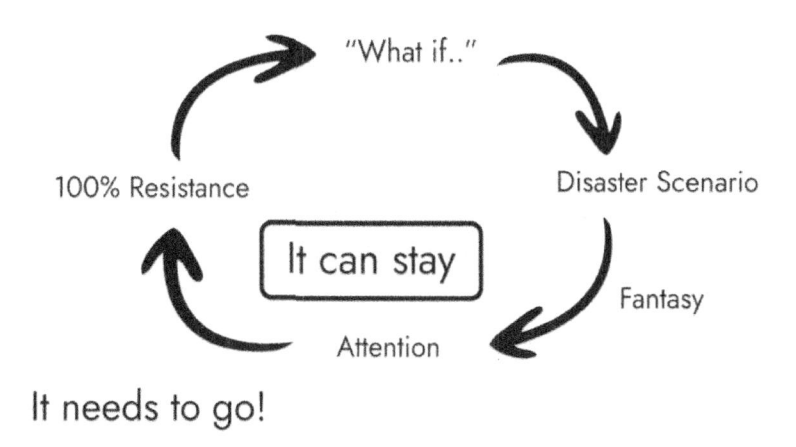

```
         "What if.."
100% Resistance        Disaster Scenario
      [ It can stay ]
                       Fantasy
         Attention
```

It needs to go!

"What if…" and disaster scenarios are not bad at all. Every person has to deal with this. Paying attention isn't necessarily a bad thing either. It's about how you pay attention. If you have the intention that it has to go, then the resistance starts. Then the misery begins. Then you start coming up with more "What if…" and disaster scenarios. And the more you do that, the harder you will resist.

SILENCE

While if you give attention with the intention that it can stay, then nothing will happen. Then there will be no "what if…" thoughts and disaster scenarios. In that respect, giving attention is therefore the crucial step. Giving attention is completely in your hands. You have 100% control over this. Even if it doesn't feel that way. You decide how much attention you give. Your brain is completely under your control. In other words:

- It needs to go
- It can stay

Those are the two choices you have. With all kinds of gradients in between.

Whether it's a panic attack, sensations, thoughts or feelings. Everything works exactly this way. That's how your brain works. Your brain doesn't know the difference between yes and no. Whether you want to think about something or not, in both cases you think about it. The only difference is that if you want to consciously think about something, you accept what comes. Anxiety Is allowed to be there. Don't curse it, admire it. Be curious. No matter how negative your thoughts are, it's ok.

Johan

Chapter 20: Common Pitfalls

Accepting your anxiety sometimes seems impossible. There are many pitfalls lurking that prevent you from accepting your anxieties. In this chapter, we'll look at the pitfalls that lurk and how you can avoid or prevent them.

Wrong intentions

This is probably the most difficult part to learn. Because nobody can really teach you how to do this. In simple words: you can't lie to yourself. You can lie to any person in the world and they might believe you but you can't trick your own mind. Your intention must be real. You can't say to yourself "Ok, bring it on" but meanwhile still fear the anxiety. That doesn't work.

Also, you should have zero expectations. Do not expect that your anxiety will go away when you apply any technique. Only observe what happens. Never apply any technique with the intention to lower your anxious thoughts or lower whatever symptom you have. Because if that is your intention, it will never work.

Not spending enough time

You can only accept anxiety through practice. With mild anxieties, it sometimes goes away by itself and there isn't much to do. My anxiety of blushing was resolved within two weeks while I had suffered from it for almost 30 years. Because I had never learned how anxiety works. I did the exact same thing every time. It wasn't until I learned to turn my thoughts around that my anxiety of blushing disappeared in a matter of weeks.

So it doesn't really matter how long you've been bothered by your anxieties. They can be accepted very quickly. However, with more severe anxieties you just need more time. It's therefore important that you do the exercises on a daily basis. If you often do them reluctantly or with the wrong intention, it will be very difficult to accept your anxieties.

I often didn't feel like doing exercises. I always had better things to do. In the meantime, I tried to get rid of my anxieties by applying accelerated techniques in my head. Once I really took the time I made much more progress.

Also, don't be afraid to spend money or go to a psychologist. Ultimately, no one cares that you suffer from anxiety or panic. You're the only one who is confronted with it every day. You are the only one who can accept your anxieties. No one else can do that for you. Other people can help you but in the end, you're the one that needs to do it. The moment I started to suffer from extreme anxiety, I immediately informed everyone I knew (colleagues, my boss, parents, friends and girlfriend). And what happened? Everyone understood. In fact, a number of colleagues told me that they also suffered from certain anxieties or are still suffering from them.

Take your time and give yourself time. If you want to learn something new, it takes time. The more things you rush through because you don't feel like it, the longer it will take you to reach your goal. It makes no sense at all to do a quick exercise. It's not the practice that will make the difference, but the intention. The exercises are not a checklist that you just need to finish. You can do an exercise every day just to do an exercise but it doesn't work that way. Take your time!

Unaware of your behavior and thinking patterns

Johan

Before you can treat your anxiety, you need to know at what exact point you start to create anxious thoughts. If you're not aware that you're creating and adding up anxious thoughts, treating it will be difficult. You need to be aware of what you're doing. Few examples:

- "I'm starting to resist again"
- "I'm having those negative thoughts again"
- "There is that feeling again"

You can even give repetitive thoughts a name. Like "There is negative Joe again, telling me I'm useless". Once you start recognizing repetitive thought patterns, you can intervene by applying the techniques you learned.

The problem of need

Needing to do something is a big problem with anxieties. With every anxiety you need to do something:

- The anxiety needs to go;
- You don't want to feel this anymore;
- I don't want these negative thoughts anymore…
- It (feeling, sensation, thought. emotions) has to go..

Think about your own thoughts, do the words "have to", "need" or "don't want" come up regularly? For me personally:

- I **have to** sleep well because otherwise, it's not good for my health..
- I **don't want** to feel this tension in my body anymore. It has to go.
- I **have to** do an exercise to get rid of the feeling.
- This feeling **needs to go**.

SILENCE

These are very powerful words. In general, people think they need to do something to get rid of their anxiety. And they try many things. Realize that your anxiety only exists because you are trying to get rid of it. You don't need to do anything at all. Change the above words in:

"I'm allowed to feel this"

- I'm allowed to sleep badly;
- I'm allowed to feel the tension;
- I'm allowed to feel this feeling or emotion;
- I don't need to do any exercise, I choose to do it to heal myself.

Looking for 100% certainty

Probably the biggest pitfall is looking for 100% certainty. The simple fact is, 100% certainty doesn't exist. You can't predict the future. Most people with anxiety are looking for 100% certainty. They want to be 100% certain that their disaster scenario can't come true.

Not being certain of what will happen makes our life interesting. Wouldn't it be boring if you already know what will happen for the rest of your life? I would advise doing research to the point you're pretty certain and then letting it go. For example, if you're afraid of getting a heart attack you can do multiple things:

- Getting checked by your doctor;
- Eating healthy;
- Exercise on a regular basis;

Other than that, there is not much you can do. Even if you do all these things you can still get a heart attack. Even if you are 100% healthy. Be aware of your thoughts and apply a technique to figure out if your thoughts are realistic.

Johan

Chapter 21: When are your anxieties resolved?

When are your anxieties resolved? How do you know that you no longer suffer from anxiety? I touched on this briefly at the end of Chapter Five. The answer is very simple. Now that you know exactly how anxiety and panic work, when are your anxieties resolved/accepted?

If you don't think about it anymore!

You can't consciously check anxieties in the moment whether they are still there. Because then they are still there. You think about it again. The realization that you're no longer bothered by your anxiety always comes **afterward** and never in the moment. So suppose you get a red face during every social encounter, when will your anxiety be resolved?

If, after the meeting, you suddenly become aware of the fact that you didn't get a red face during the meeting. You don't care anymore. As long as you keep checking whether you are still afraid of something, you still fear your disaster scenario. Because if you're not anxious anymore, why are you still checking to see if it's still there?

SILENCE

Have you ever consciously experienced falling asleep? Did you ever had the exact thought:

> "Oh yes, now I'm falling asleep"

That is impossible. Because you can only sleep when your brain is no longer consciously thinking. Although there are techniques that teach you how to lucid dream and then you actually can consciously fall asleep. But normally, the logical part of your brain is turned off when you fall asleep. It's an automatic process. The only reason you fall asleep is when our brain has settled down and you're not consciously thinking about anything. People who worry before going to sleep therefore have a hard time falling asleep. Because you can't sleep until you stop thinking. People who worry, are thinking all the time.

The dizziness I experienced (mentioned in chapter five) is a good example. I was completely distracted from my dizziness while talking to an old friend because I was no longer consciously engaged in thinking about my dizziness. Only at that moment, I was not aware of it. My attention was somewhere else. Only **after** the conversation was over did I realize (consciously) that I hadn't been dizzy for 30 minutes. If I consciously checked during the conversation whether I was still dizzy, I would immediately become dizzy. Because consciously checking whether the anxiety/sensation is still there is precisely the problem!

So how do you know your anxiety has resolved? If you are no longer consciously concerned with your anxiety in the situation where you're normally anxious. So don't feel it anymore, think about it, check if it's still there etc. You only know afterward that it doesn't bother you anymore.

21.1 Your anxiety will come back one day

Either way, there will come a time in your life when your anxiety will come back. Once you've experienced something, it stays in

Johan

your memory for the rest of your life. There will come a time when you suddenly think about your anxiety again. That happened to me. I literally didn't think about my anxiety in any way for several years. Due to a combination of circumstances, my anxiety came back again. And this time even worse than before.

But next time you're prepared for this. The techniques in this book will last a lifetime. The next time your anxiety shows itself again, you immediately know what to do. Anxiety is part of life. Never being anxious again can therefore never be a goal. Realize that your anxiety can always come back.

SILENCE

Summary Theme 3

In theme 3 you learned how to investigate your thought patterns and behavior. You used this information in the various techniques to deal with anxiety and panic. Other emotions might also be in the way like sadness or anger.

You've learned several techniques to accept your anxiety. We also looked at possible pitfalls when accepting your anxieties. You also learned how to recognize when your anxiety is gone. And most importantly, common pitfalls that are lurking in the shadow that prevent you from accepting your anxiety.
Theme 4 : Useful tips and things to avoid

In this theme I'll go into more detail about useful tips and things to avoid. I'll discuss how medication works and natural alternatives. In addition, we'll have a look at the influence of nutrition on anxiety. As a bonus, I go deeper into the Wim Hof technique and how it can help with anxiety.

Johan

Chapter 22: Medication

Medication is a controversial topic. I'm not a doctor or scientist. I can't give you all the details about how medication works. What I do know is that there are many thousands of chemicals in your brain that are responsible for who you are (your ego), what kind of thoughts you have and how that creates your personality. How you were raised and how your parents behave also have a major influence on who you are as a person.

First an important disclaimer: if you are currently taking medication, only consult a professional about the next step. Never just stop taking medication and never just take extra medication without consultation.

The fact is that it has never been scientifically proven that people with anxiety and panic lack substances (neurotransmitters) in the brain. That doesn't sound logical at all. Then no one would be able to solve anxiety and panic without medication. But neurotransmitters do influence our behaviors. So the scientific hypothesis is that if someone is not feeling well and this lasts for a very long time (years), there must be something wrong with neurotransmitters in your brain. But how exactly does that work for people who have never suffered from anxiety or panic and suddenly develop anxiety symptoms due to an event? In my case, I went from no anxiety to severe anxiety in just 24 hours.

SILENCE

Medication can help, but will never solve the underlying problem. You can think of medication as swimming rings. It can help and support you very well. But at some point, the swimming rings have to come off. Although, some people need swimming rings all their lives. That's totally fine. Just keep in mind that medication can produce severe side effects.

Medication works in the same way as drugs. Actually, medication is just drugs but in a medically "responsible" way. In Chapter 14, we talked about increasing your limits with drugs. Medication does not increase your limit but weakens your limit.

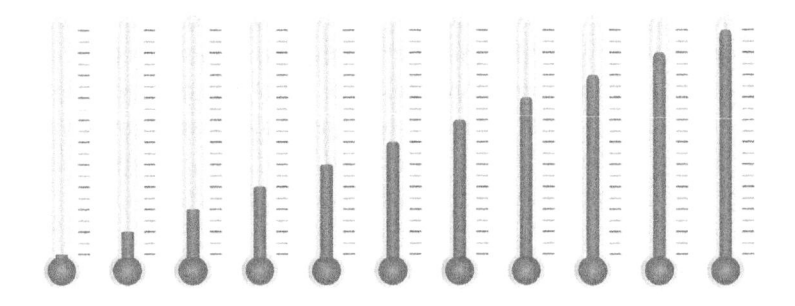

As a human being, you can feel emotions from 0 to 100. Where you feel nothing at 0 and are extremely happy or anxious at 100. Drugs can increase the limit of emotions to 200. A good example of this is ecstasy.

Ecstasy ensures, among other things, that all serotonin in your brain is released at once. In addition, the serotonin reserves are also addressed. It also contains substances that ensure that the reuptake of serotonin by the nerves is blocked. The result is that you have an unnatural amount of "happy substances" in your brain for hours. As a result, you'll be in the happiest mood for hours on end. Everyone is your best friend, anxiety no longer exists and you feel super relaxed.

Johan

You'll never be able to experience this feeling naturally. Think about the time in your life when you were happiest. Multiply this moment five times and you'll have an idea of what it feels like to use ecstasy. Incidentally, not everyone experiences the same effect. That shows once again that in theory neurotransmitters have an influence on how you feel but every person reacts differently. Some people don't feel any effect after taking ecstasy. Just as well that there are people who don't benefit at all from medication.

Medication does the opposite. It doesn't increase the limit to 200 but lowers the limit of your emotions to 80. A common "complaint" among medication users is that it feels like emotions have been flattened. Medication doesn't only affect anxiety. Medication affects <u>all</u> emotions. Because the limit of anxiety can no longer exceed 80, you're better capable of handling anxious thoughts. But your other emotions are also limited to 80.

However, medication results differ per person. Sometimes you have to use different types of medication to see which one works best. This is of course highly undesirable because there are negative consequences. In general, medication only works well for moderate to severe anxiety symptoms. It's really not advisable to use medication for mild anxiety symptoms in any form.

Many different types of drugs are prescribed for anxiety and panic. Especially different types of benzodiazepines:

- Diazepam
- Oxazepam
- Flurazepam
- Lorazepam
- Nitrazepam
- etc.

SILENCE

These benzodiazepines are intended to calm you down by releasing GABA in the brain. This can be helpful with sudden constant anxieties. Or when falling asleep. But because these drugs only work for a short time and are highly addictive, they can only be used for a maximum of a few weeks. In some cases two months. After that, you really have to get rid of them. These drugs do not solve your anxiety and you become addicted to them after prolonged use. They're also less effective with longer use. But sometimes it's just necessary.

Don't confuse this with GABA found in so-called "GABA" supplements. These supplements tell you that it increases GABA in the brain but GABA can't cross the blood brain barrier so those supplements will never reach our brain.

Taking medication is certainly not wrong or bad as long as you don't use it for prolonged periods of time. The longer you are on medication, the more difficult it will become to stop taking them. Therefore, never let yourself be prescribed medication without reason. Psychologists and doctors are very down-to-earth about it. Before you know it you will be on medication when you don't really need it. Medication is the very last step in any treatment. Only in severe cases, medication should be described.

Johan

Chapter 23. Natural Alternatives to Medication

There is often a bit of laughter about alternative medicine. The fact is that alternative medicine is scientifically proven effective. The Western medical industry is not the holy grail but only part of the whole.

It makes sense that the pharmaceutical industry isn't going to spend billions testing herbs that anyone can buy anywhere. They won't make much profit selling low-cost herbs. Many people forget that the main goal of pharmaceutical companies is not to cure people, but to make money. They are commercial companies. For example, did you know that they literally spend many billions on marketing? That general practitioners and other doctors can receive a commission if they prescribe drug X? That's simply how this industry works. They also won't do anything in preventing you from getting sick but only sell you products (medicine) when you do get sick.

The reason I mention this is that there are plenty of people who label alternative medicine as bullshit. It's quackery, doesn't work and the Western medical world is the holy grail. However, many people don't know that many medicines are not effective, only treat the symptoms, and are based on the placebo effect.

SILENCE

There are literally hundreds of thousands of stories to be found of people who have been naturally cured of all kinds of diseases by using alternative medicine or simply eating different foods. People who had been written off by the Western medical world. If you are anti-alternative medicine, I will of course not just change your mindset with a few lines of text. Even if you don't believe in it at all, give it a chance. It costs you almost nothing and can help and support you enormously with your anxiety.

Just as with medicine, not all natural alternatives have the desired effect. One person feels nothing at all and the other benefits greatly. Testing it out to see if it's beneficial for you is my advice.

Disclaimer: do not use alternative herbs if you are taking medication. Herbs can influence the effect of medication. Only do this in consultation with a doctor.

23.1 Anti-stress - Ashwagandha

Ashwagandha is an herb from the nightshade family. The root of Ashwagandha is used as a remedy for many different ailments. Ashwagandha is an adaptogen.

Quote from Wikipedia:

"Adaptogens or adaptogenic substances, compounds or herbs refer to the pharmacological concept where administration results in stabilization of physiological processes and the promotion of homeostasis, e.g. reduced cellular sensitivity to stress. The term 'adaptogenic' is often used to describe treatments that can increase the resistance of the organism to biological stress in experimental and clinical studies."

Various scientific studies* have shown that Ashwagandha has a positive influence on the following:

- Improving overall fitness

- Anti-aging
- Recovery after illness
- Acute and chronic stress
- Helps with stress-related complaints and disorders: anxiety, restlessness, depression, learning and memory problems, insomnia, weight loss,
- Improve cognition, mental focus and memory
- Helps with chronic fatigue
- Helps with Alzheimer's disease, Parkinson's disease, Huntington's disease
- Helps with a lowered libido
- Helps with reduced fertility (men)
- Helps with premenstrual syndrome
- Helps with menopausal complaints
- Helps with muscle weakness, sarcopenia
- Helps with osteoarthritis, rheumatoid arthritis, gout
- Helps with diabetes
- Promotes growth and development in adolescents
- Protection against cardiovascular disease
- Helps with Gastrointestinal infections

Ashwagandha does a lot of positive things in your body. In addition to all the above benefits, Ashwagandha can reduce cortisol (stress hormone) up to 30%. So if you are under a lot of stress, it's important to give your body a rest. If you are anxious, you're unable to relax. Ashwagandha can help with this.

My personal experience with Ashwagandha is that it definitely helps with stress management. I really feel less stressed throughout the day and it helps with sleep.

 * Scientific sources:

1. Singh N et al. An overview of ashwagandha: a rejuvenator of ayurveda. Afr J Tradit Complement Alternate With. 2011;8(5S):208-213.

2. Mishra LC et al. Scientific basis for the therapeutic use of Withania somnifera (ashwagandha): a review. Altern Med Rev. 2000;5(4):334-46.

3. Chandrasekhar K et al. A prospective, randomized double-blind, placebo-controlled study of safety and efficacy of a high-concentration full-spectrum extract of ashwagandha root in reducing stress and anxiety in adults. Indian J Psychol Med. 2012;34(3):255-62.

4. Pratte MA et al. An alternative treatment for anxiety: a systematic review of human trial results reported for the Ayurvedic herb ashwagandha (Withania somnifera). J Altern Complement Med. 2014;20(12):901-8.

5. Pingali U et al. Effect of standardized aqueous extract of Withania somnifera on tests of cognitive and psychomotor performance in healthy human participants. Pharmacognosy Res. 2014;6(1):12-18.

6. Kuboyama T et al. Effects of Ashwagandha (roots of Withania somnifera) on neurodegenerative diseases. Biol Pharm Bull. 2014;37(6):892-7.

[PubMed] 7. Dries DR et al. Extracting β-amyloid from Alzheimer's disease. Proc Natl Acad Sci USA 2012;109(9):3199-200.

8. Raghavan A et al. Withaniasomnifera: a pre-clinical study on neuroregenerative therapy for stroke. Neural Regen Res. 2015;10(2):183-5.

9. Dongre S et al. Efficacy and Safety of Ashwagandha (Withania somnifera) Root Extract in Improving Sexual Function in Women: A Pilot Study. Biomed Res Int. 2015;2015:284154.

10. Mahdi AA et al. Withaniasomnifera improves semen quality in stress-related male fertility. Evid Based Complement Alternat Med. 2011;2011:576962.

11. Raut AA et al. Exploratory study to evaluate tolerability, safety, and activity of Ashwagandha (Withania somnifera) in healthy volunteers. J Ayurveda Integr Med. 2012;3(3):111-4

23.2 Curcumin - Turmeric - Curcuma

Turmeric (also called yellow root) is a well-known herb that is mainly used in the kitchen. For example, think of yellow rice. Yellow rice is simply white rice but processed with turmeric extract. You see yellow rice a lot in the Indian kitchen.

In addition to being a widely used herb in the kitchen, turmeric also has many beneficial healing powers. Turmeric is known to be one of the most powerful herbs in the world. It's full of antioxidants and anti-inflammatory. It is widely used to treat various diseases and has many beneficial effects:

- Reduces oxidation and inflammation
- Reduces metabolic syndrome
- Reduces arthritis
- Reduces anxiety and depression
- Helps with hyperlipidemia (to many fats in the bloodstream)
- Reduces muscle strain
- Preventing and treating cancer
- Improved brain functions
- Lowers risk of brain-related diseases (Alzheimer's etc).
- Lowers risk of cardiovascular disease

The advantage is that you can buy it in any Asian store. Most of the products you see online are pills with turmeric extract. However, these pills are shockingly expensive compared to a bag of turmeric from a specialized Asian store. For a bag of turmeric powder of 1000 grams, you pay about €20 in my country. For a jar of 90 pills (600 mg) you pay an average of €24.

It's important to note that turmeric is absorbed much better if you take it together with black pepper. In fact, every turmeric supplement should contain black pepper. If you buy a bag of turmeric powder yourself, buy a bag of black pepper immediately. It is even better to combine both with unsaturated fatty acids. Like olive oil or linseed oil.

Some scientific studies:

- www.healthline.com/nutrition/top-10-evidence-based-health-benefits-of-turmeric#TOC_TITLE_HDR_10
- https://www.ncbi.nlm.nih.gov/pmc/articles/PMC3918523/

23.3 Passionflower

Passionflower is a well-known herb that is mainly used as a sedative. It is often used for:

- Inner turmoil
- Nervousness
- Stress
- Irritability
- Anxiety
- Exhaustion
- Headache
- Backache
- Tensions
- Insomnia

Most people use passionflower to make bedtime tea. Due to the calming effect, worrying thoughts are less present and you fall asleep earlier. It also promotes a good night's sleep and ensures a better recovery of body and mind. Passionflower, like ashwagandha, is an adaptogen. For 1000 grams of passion flower you pay about €25 euros and you can use it for months.

23.4 Lemon balm

Lemon balm (lemon balm) has the same beneficial effects as passion flower. Lemon balm and passionflower are therefore often taken together. This combination gives you extra peace of mind. Mainly taken at bedtime.

23.5 Vitamin D

Vitamin D is one of the most important vitamins that we need as humans. Many people have low vitamin D levels. Your body gets vitamin D from sunlight and specific foods such as oily fish. Although it's great to go outdoors in the Netherlands during the summer, we are quickly indoors in the fall and winter. And if we go outside during this period, we are thickly dressed.

Most people don't get out enough. And the vast majority are not really fish eaters either. A vitamin D deficiency can therefore quickly arise. Vitamin D plays an important role in many processes in the body. It has also been shown that a too-low vitamin D level can influence anxiety and panic.

The best option to make enough vitamin D is to be outdoors for at least 30 minutes every day. Supplemented with vitamin D from food. Think of oily fish or to a lesser extent from meat and eggs. Vitamin D is also often added to butter (low-fat spreads).

Additional supplementation is also possible. Then choose vitamin D3 (not D2). D3 is better absorbed by our bodies. Pills or other things are full of junk such as additives and sweeteners. The best vitamin D3 supplement is called Cholecalciferol and the only added ingredient should be olive oil. Please note that too much vitamin D can be harmful.

23.6 Omega 3

Omega 3 is a very important type of fat that has a lot of influence on various processes in our body. Omega 3 protects, among other things, the brain and ensures a healthy heart. Omega 3 can also influence your anxiety symptoms. Omega 3 consists of EPA and DHA fatty acids. There is also a vegetable version of omega 3 called ALA. ALA is converted into EPA and DHA in our bodies. But this is much less effective.

Omega 3 can't be produced by your body and must therefore be obtained from food or supplements. EPA and DHA Omega 3 fats are mainly found in oily fish. Think of herring, mackerel or salmon. Since most people don't eat fish, you might get deficient in omega-3 fats. You can supplement this with ALA from linseed oil. ALA is converted to EPA and DHA for about 9%. So that is not very effective. But better than nothing at all. ALA is mainly found in linseed oil and chia seeds.

An alternative is to take supplementation. However, this can become expensive in the long run. Omega 3 supplements are not very cheap. There are some scientific studies that show that omega 3 can help with anxiety.

- https://www.health.harvard.edu/blog/omega-3-fatty-acids-for-mood-disorders-2018080314414
- https://www.healio.com/news/psychiatry/20180914/omega3-fatty-acids-may-help-ease-anxiety-symptoms
- https://medicalxpress.com/news/2011-07-omega-anxiety-inflammation-healthy-students.html

23.7 Probiotics

It has been scientifically proven that there is a connection between gut flora and mental health. By often eating processed foods, your intestinal flora will adapt to them. This creates an unhealthy balance between good and bad bacteria.

Johan

Probiotics restore the balance between good and bad bacteria through an overload of good bacteria.

By far the best probiotic you can take is kefir made from organic milk straight from a goat. For this you need:

- Kefir grains
- A glass jar with a plastic lid
- Organic goat's milk (unpasteurized)

1) Put 2 teaspoons of kefir in the jar. Fill the jar with goat's milk. Make sure the jar is not completely full (leave 3 cm to the lid).
2) Put the lid loosely on the jar. Do not tighten it all the way
3) Place the jar in a warm place out of sunlight for 24 hours.
4) The kefir is ready when the milk has thickened a bit and smells fermented (a bit like buttermilk).
5) Close the lid tightly and shake vigorously
6) Pour the kefir into another jar or glass. Use a sieve to collect the kefir grains. With the kefir grains that remain, you start again at step 1.

What is also important to know:

Sugar is very bad for your good bacteria. Therefore, avoid sugar from your diet as much as possible. Sugar and anxiety don't go well together. Just be aware of what your body needs. If you sit on the couch watching television for a few hours, your body doesn't need much energy. So eating chips or drinking sugary drinks wreaks havoc in your body.

However, when you just did a very intensive workout, it's best to get at least 50 grams of sugar to help your muscles recover. You only need a high amount of sugar before, during or after an intensive workout. Sugar isn't bad for your health, as long as it's in tune with your body's activity level. Did you know pro cyclists that participated in the tour the France live several years longer on average versus "normal" people? Meanwhile, pro cyclists consume multiple times more sugar than a normal person in their lives. In other words, consuming large amounts of sugar is fine if your body needs it. But it's known that sugar isn't helping with anxiety and probably worsens it.

Tip: Kefir from the supermarket is not real kefir. This is made with pasteurized milk from which all good bacteria have already disappeared (due to the heating). You can only make real kefir yourself or buy it somewhere that you know for sure is real kefir.

- https://www.sciencedirect.com/science/article/abs/pii/S0165178119312156

Other natural probiotic options include:

- Sauerkraut;
- Kimchi;
- Raw cheese;
- In supplement form (make sure that as many different strains of bacteria as possible are present).

The ultimate bedtime cocktail

The best time to take these natural herbs is before sleep. During your sleep, your brain is extra active and your body is being repaired. The perfect time to give your body and mind a helping hand.

My evening cocktail looked like this:

- Passionflower tea (sometimes supplemented with lemon balm)
- 2-3 grams turmeric + black pepper + linseed oil

- 0.5 - 1 gram of Ashwagandha
- Few drops of vitamin d3

Try out a combination yourself. But be careful not to combine this with medication.

Chapter 24: Influence of diet on anxiety

Although food or certain drinks can certainly influence your anxiety, it's unlikely that this is the root cause of your anxiety. It's often a combination of many conditions and not a single type of food or drink. But according to scientific studies, it can affect your mental health.

Just go through the list of foods below. Maybe there is something in this list that you eat or drink on a daily basis. You can then make the decision to stop eating it for a month or two and check if this has any influence on your mental state.

Foods with a positive effect on anxiety:

- Spinach (large amounts of magnesium)
- Pumpkin seeds
- Berries
- Avocados
- Chia and flax seed (oil)
- Oatmeal
- Turmeric / Kurkuma
- Brazilian nuts
- Chickpeas
- Dark chocolate

Foods with a negative effect on anxiety:

SILENCE

- Sugar
- Trans fats (fries, chips, pizza, cookies, etc.)
- Energy drinks
- Artificial sweeteners (aspartame, acesulfame-k, sucralose)
- Milk products
- Refined carbohydrates (white bread, white pasta, white rice, etc).
- Processed meat (salami, sausage, etc)
- Alcohol
- Gluten

The chance is almost 100% that you eat something from the list of foods with a negative effect every day. Replace all the bad things with foods from the positive list. In combination with alternative herbs (see chapter 21). Then you have a very powerful combination. This combination is not only positive for your anxiety but for your entire body.

My personal diet looks like this:

In the morning:

- Immediately after getting up a glass of water with sea salt(200ml)

Around 10:00:

- Oatmeal + spelled flakes
- Vacant
- Blueberries
- Banana
- Cinnamon powder
- Pure cocoa powder
- Flaxseed oil
- 200 to 300 ml of water

Johan

At noon:

- Spinach (raw)
- 3 eggs
- Pickle
- Cucumber
- Red onion
- Broccoli (raw)
- Sweet potato
- Carrot
- Paprika

Later on the day:

- 2/4 whole wheat buns with peanut butter.

Evening meal:

- Generally vegetables plus meat (chicken).

Before bedtime:

- Passionflower tea
- 2-3 grams of turmeric + black pepper
- 0.5 - 1 gram of Ashwagandha
- Few drops of vitamin d3

I do eat junk food from time to time. Bag of chips, pizza, fries, cookies, etc. Stop eating bad things altogether is the best thing you can do. But also by far the most difficult. Just make a habit of eating healthy 5-6 days a week minimum and one day a week you can eat some of the bad stuff without any problems.

24.1 Vegetarian, fasting and keto (meat only)

If you want to take it up a notch, you can decide to change your diet entirely. You can become a vegetarian, only eat meat and fats (keto) and incorporate fasting. There are many people who have cured their anxiety and depression by fully changing their diets.

Now I can probably write a complete book on these subjects so I won't cover too much in this book. What I do want to mention is that you should incorporate fasting no matter your current diet. Fasting means you stop eating for a specific period of time. This can be an entire day once a week or 16 hours a day. I'm currently following an intermittent fasting plan that allows me to eat between 10:00 am and 18:00 p.m. So I always have a 16-hour window of not eating every day. Fasting has a lot of benefits. Mainly stopping insulin spikes which are caused by eating carbs and helping your body to clean up cells.

Fasting can also help reduce anxiety symptoms caused by insulin spikes and eating too many carbs. You can also try a keto diet which consists mostly of fats and protein. This ensures you won't have any insulin spikes and your body gets its energy from ketones instead of glucose.

24.2 Physical complaints due to nutrition

You may be allergic to certain foods without knowing it. This can cause physical sensations. And that can lead to anxiety complaints. For example, if you have a hidden allergy and you have been suffering from physical sensations for years and the doctor can't find anything, you can start worrying that you have to live with it for the rest of your life.

If you suffer from physical sensations or chronic pain and you can't find a cause, it may well be due to nutrition. First, make a basic overview of all the foods and drinks you consume each day. Replace a product from the negative list with something from the positive list. Don't replace everything at once but per product. Then eat according to this new pattern for a month or two. Do this until you have replaced all negative products with positive ones. Meanwhile, write down how you feel each week.

By replacing a negative product every month, you can eventually rule out that food is the cause of your sensations. You can also change your diet all at once. But this is very difficult to maintain. In addition, you do not know which product is causing your complaints.

Chapter 25: What's Best to Avoid?

People with anxiety invent rituals, actions, and all kinds of ways to control their anxiety. But as you know by now you can't control an emotion. If you try to control it, it will have consequences. In this chapter, we'll look at things to avoid if you have anxiety.

Stop searching the internet…

People with anxiety, panic and depressive symptoms are always looking for solutions to solve their problems. And their journey starts on the big bad internet. Can you find the solution on the internet? Absolutely. But it can also make your complaints ten times worse. The more fuel you give the anxiety and panic, the worse the complaints will become. Chances are the internet will exacerbate these negative thoughts rather than fix them.

On the other hand, it is very natural to look for a solution to your anxiety problems. But if you don't understand exactly how anxiety works and what actions make it worse instead of better, the internet will probably only make your complaints worse. Chances are small that you'll suddenly get rid of your anxiety by reading a few articles on the internet. Unfortunately, it doesn't work that way. I've read the entire internet to find a solution.

The first practical tip: STOP looking for a solution on the internet.

- Stop reading stories about people who are depressed or have anxiety issues.
- Stop reading forums/blogs about anxiety.
- Stop looking for a solution to your anxiety problem.

All this does is that you continuously acknowledge that you have a problem that you need to solve. But there is nothing to solve, that's the whole problem! Anxiety does not exist if you don't try to solve it!

Because you constantly think you have to solve your anxiety, it remains a part of your life. Your anxiety only exists because you give it attention. The more negative attention you give (try to solve) the worse the complaints become. It's impossible to run away from it or suppress anxiety. Anxiety is part of the human body. Embrace it.

Rituals and the Placebo Effect

A well-known phenomenon is the placebo effect. Someone is given a fake medicine (medicine without active substances) but still feels pain relief. This is called the placebo effect. Studies have shown that many medicines mainly rely on the placebo effect and actually don't work for the majority of people.

Suppose you are on medication to control your anxiety and panic. The next time the pharmacist gives you a box of fake medicines, but you don't know this. They are just like the medicines you always take. You'll notice that something changes because you no longer take effective medicines. But you won't instantly relate this to your medicine.

Johan

But now imagine the following situation:

Situation 1:

You go on vacation and (without knowing it) you get a box of fake medicines. During your holiday you feel a bit strange. Logical, because your medicines no longer work. However, you don't know this, so you don't give it much attention.

Situation 2:
You go on vacation and (without knowing it) you get a box of fake medicines. Immediately on the first day after arriving at the holiday destination, your partner tells you that you have been given fake medicines.

What will happen in situation 2? You'll probably panic right away because you'll be out of medication for the entire holiday. Your whole vacation falls apart. While in situation 1 you have exactly the same circumstances. But because you are convinced (you really believe it) that you have your normal medicines you worry a lot less.

In extreme cases, there are women who are completely convinced that they are pregnant. Their whole body produces exactly the same hormones that are part of a normal pregnancy. While they are not pregnant at all. That is the power of believing in your own thoughts. And as you know, that can also have very nasty consequences. Right now, you still believe in your anxious thoughts.

Therefore, try to skip a ritual (if you have a ritual). I know from personal experience that this can be very difficult. I used certain herbs to help me sleep. If I didn't use these, I often didn't sleep well. My bedtime ritual of taking herbs perpetuated my anxiety about not being able to sleep well. Once I slowly started to reduce this ritual, I started to notice that I do sleep well without

SILENCE

using herbs. At some point, I realized that my sleep is much less dependent on herbs than I initially thought.

Your rituals are placebo effects. They might work very well but only because you think they do. The problem is that every ritual you use is a reminder of your anxiety. Because you simply wouldn't use rituals if you didn't suffer from anxiety.

Breathing techniques and meditation
In short, whatever breathing technique you use isn't going to change your thinking in the long term. It can make you calmer the moment you perform the exercise. People often breathe too quickly and shallowly. Your brain/body thinks there is danger. You can stop this signal with certain breathing techniques. However, that doesn't make your disaster scenarios or "what if" thoughts suddenly disappear. But it can work wonders while having a panic attack or when trying to fall asleep. So it's more a temporary solution than a real fix. You can still do breathing techniques but just remind yourself that it won't solve your anxiety. It's actually a trigger because you wouldn't be doing any breathing techniques if you weren't anxious. Instead of applying a breathing technique, I would recommend inviting unwanted thoughts and feelings and trying to greet them.

And the same thing is true for meditation practices. This is a made up number by myself but I think 95% of all people practicing mediation had some event preceding this. By that I mean something happened in their lives and read about meditation and how that can work wonders for mental issues and overall well being. I took a full mindfulness course. From the 20 attendees, there was only 1 person out of curiosity. All others had all kinds of mental problems (including me). Even the teacher started meditation because of some events that happened years ago.

So, simply ask yourself the following question:

Johan

> "Would I also do breathing exercises or meditation if I <u>didn't suffer</u> from anxiety or panic?"

If the answer is "no" then simply stop. It won't help you. Because then it becomes a way of trying to get rid of your problem. If the answer is "yes" please continue!

Chapter 26. Bonus: the Wim Hof technique

You may have heard the name "The Iceman". Wim "the iceman" Hof was in a bad mental state after the loss of his wife (suicide). Wim went looking for a way to give him some relief. Wim has found a unique combination of breathing techniques and exposure to cold that makes him almost invincible. Did you know that Wim Hof:

- Can sit up to the neck in a container of ice for almost 2 hours;
- Climbed Mount Everest in just underpants;
- Climbed Mount Kilimanjaro in just underpants;
- Ran a marathon in Finland at -20 degrees in just underpants;
- Ran a marathon in the desert without drinking water;
- Can hold his breath for 10 minutes;
- Wim can consciously influence his own hormones;

And the list goes on and on. If there is anyone on this planet who can carry the term "superman" it's Wim Hof. Now you may

SILENCE

think ok, that's all well and good, but how can that help me? The beauty of the Wim Hof technique is that you can learn it yourself!

That doesn't mean you should run a marathon in the desert or at -20 on the arctic circle, but you can use this technique to make you almost immortal mentally and physically. If you apply the Wim Hof technique, you will literally never get sick with the flu again. This has even been scientifically researched. Wim and a number of people he trained in 10 weeks injected themselves with e Coli (a bacteria that makes you very ill) and no one who followed his training got sick. While all the people in the control group did get sick.
Scientific research:

https://www.pnas.org/content/111/20/7379.full

Despite this, you can of course still be skeptical about the results. I have used the Wim Hof technique myself and still use it. The technique consists of special breathing exercises and exposure to cold (cold shower). Before I started the Wim Hof technique, I became ill quite often (at least 3 times a year). And by sick, I mean that I really had to lie in bed to recover and couldn't work or exercise. Especially since the birth of my first child, I noticed that I started to get sick more often.

I have been using the Wim Hof technique for about 1.5 years now and have never been ill since. Maybe a sniffling nose. While my girlfriend and son are still sick quite often. You are training your immune system. Due to the specific breathing techniques, your body is flooded with loads of oxygen. No bacteria or other diseases can survive in an oxygen-rich environment. So an infection doesn't stand a chance. In addition, certain hormones are released that help the body to fight off infections.

Cold shower prepares your body. We humans are actually very lazy and used to warm environments. When do you really come into contact with the cold? If it's cold outside, we put on warm clothes. If it's cold inside we turn on the heating. Our body is no longer used to the cold at all. By taking a cold shower every day you train your immune system. And yes, taking a cold shower is a challenge. But once you get used to it, it's not that cold at all.

But the only reason it's a challenge is because…? You are thinking about it!

What does this have to do with anxiety? If you are afraid of the coronavirus or suffer from anxiety about contamination or getting sick, you can use this technique to give yourself a mental and physical boost. It has been scientifically proven that after using this technique people hardly ever get sick from the flu. Corona (Covid-19) will also have much less chance. So if you are very afraid of corona and its possible consequences, this is the perfect technique.

Now I'm guessing that one of the following thoughts has crossed your mind:

- "Cold shower? I'm really not going to do that…"
- "My body can't stand the cold"
- "I can't take a cold shower"
- "I'm really not going to take a cold shower because…"

Become aware of the thoughts you have. Are these thoughts true or are you making excuses not to take a cold shower? This is a great example of your brain coming up with all sorts of ways to avoid taking a cold shower. 99.99% of all people on this earth can take a cold shower without any problem. Are you one of the 0.01% who is not allowed to take a cold shower due to an illness or condition or are you just making excuses not to do it?

It must be mentioned that the Wim Hof method changed many lives. Many people who suffered from anxiety or depression are now symptom free. It might be due to the fact that during cold

SILENCE

showers and breathing exercises, you have no time to think. The breathing gives you a temporarily high feeling and the cold makes you super alert and awake. The complete Wim Hof course lasts 10-12 weeks and costs $100 up to $400.

If you are doing any meditation exercises, I would recommend doing a Wim Hof breathing technique prior to the meditation. This way you start your meditation way more relaxed and you reach a meditative state of mind easier.

I'm aware that I mentioned in the previous chapter that breathing techniques won't help you solve anxiety because your thoughts won't change in the long term when doing a breathing technique. However, many people did see benefits when combining it with cold therapy. It didn't help me but it certainly might help you. So if you are curious, just try it out!

You don't need to purchase the entire course, start with the following video:

https://www.youtube.com/watch?v=0BNejY1e9ik&t=6s&ab_channel=WimHof

I just want to mention this: I saw some news reports of Wim Hof getting sued because some people died using his techniques. Yes, it's true. Some people actually died. But that has nothing to do with the method itself but because these people did the breathing exercises in water. Because these exercises can cause you to faint, you should never ever do the breathing exercises near or in water.

Johan

Chapter 27: In Practice

You'll not stop the anxiety program from running by reading books, watching videos or talking to a psychologist. You can only stop the anxiety program through **action**. By applying everything you have learned in this book in practice. The only way to accept anxiety is through repetition. So that your automatic response to a certain thought or event slowly changes.

A reminder of the key insights in this book:

- You are not alone, there are hundreds; of millions of people with anxiety;
- You are not stupid or crazy;
- Anxiety has nothing to do with too few neurotransmitters in your brain. You're totally fine;
- Stopping trying to solve the problem is the only way to really "solve" anxiety;
- Have a clear goal. Never feeling your anxiety again can never be the goal;
- Anxiety is a circle of "What if", disaster scenarios, attention and resistance;
- Anxiety is always a fantasy and does not come true in 99.99% of cases;
- Panic is 100% anxiety. Panic is 100% resistance;
- You can't consciously accept anxiety in the moment. Just as well that you can't consciously fall asleep;
- Anxiety is 100% accepted once you stop thinking about it;
- Medication never solves your anxiety and only treats the symptoms;
- Medication puts a limit on all emotions, not just anxiety;
- Use various herbs as an alternative to medication;
- Diet can affect your anxiety;
- Apply and test the different techniques and variations in this book;

- Avoid searching the internet for a solution or reading stories from others;
- Stop using rituals. They remind you of your anxiety.

The most common anxieties:

- Spiders
- Heights/flying
- Driving
- Social
- Thunder
- Agoraphobia
- Claustrophobia

These anxieties can be subdivided into different shapes and sizes. For example, someone with anxiety about driving can become anxious if he/she has to drive through a tunnel. The other is afraid to cause an accident and another is afraid to cross a bridge. There are literally millions of variations.

Anxiety about spiders

The most common anxiety in the Netherlands is anxiety about spiders. Anxiety about spiders and other insects is fairly logical. This anxiety is more in our DNA than, for example, social anxiety. Because we lived in the jungle not so long ago. Exotic spiders and insects can be deadly so it is not surprising that we are extra alert to them. In addition, they also look scary with eight eyes and ten legs.

Every anxiety starts with "what if". If you are afraid of spiders, you may not be afraid of the spider, but what might happen if the spider walks on your hand. For example, by thinking that the spider is going to bite and that it's going to hurt. Or that you think the spider is poisonous and that you will die. The technique you can use here:

SILENCE

- Debunk your catastrophic thoughts

Is what you think correct? Is that really true?

- Do you really die if a spider bites you?
- Can spiders that occur in the Netherlands bite at all?
- Suppose they can bite, does that really hurt?

Of course, you can tailor the questions to your own disaster scenario. If you are afraid that a spider will bite as soon as you handle it, you can look up if spiders in your country can actually bite (most can't). After you have figured this out, you can gradually apply exposure:

- For example, you will first watch videos about spiders;
- Then you look at them from a distance in real life;
- Next time, look closer;
- The last step is that you let a small spider walk on your hand

There are special treatments that can help you with anxiety and mostly work within 24 hours.

Anxiety about heights and flying

Another anxiety that is also in our DNA is the fear of heights. If you fall from a great height you will almost certainly die. Your body and mind know that. There is hardly anyone in the world who is not afraid or frightened of great heights.

I suffer from anxiety about heights myself. The high diving board in the swimming pool was not an option for me. I avoid anything that has to do with height as much as possible. Because anxiety about heights is in your DNA, it's also harder to accept. It goes against nature a bit. Nevertheless, you can make it a lot more pleasant for yourself.

Johan

I also have a construction failure phobia. I was always afraid that the construction would give way and I would fall down into the depths. A number of examples:

- Wing breaks off, plane crashes;
- The glass floor in the Eiffel Tower breaks while I'm standing on it;
- The cable of the elevator breaks as soon as I'm in the elevator;
- The bolt that holds the tray to the cable car breaks down
- etc.

Anxiety about heights and anxiety about flying starts with exposure. You'll have to get on a plane at some point to overcome your anxiety. The most important step here is that you take it one step at a time. So that you gradually let go of control. Because the simple fact is that you have no control at all on the plane. And that is also a big part of the anxiety of flying. You have no control over the plane and you have nowhere to go.

What's the worst that could happen? That the plane crashes and that you die.

Two techniques work very well for this:

- Debunk catastrophic thoughts (is this really true?)
- Accept the outcome. It's OK.

If you are going to disprove catastrophic thoughts, you will look for evidence. Evidence for your disaster scenario. What is the probability of a plane crashing? Every plane that has crashed has ensured that this can't happen again with the next plane. A lot has to go wrong for a plane to crash.

If debunking your catastrophic thoughts doesn't help, it's best to go to the core of your anxiety. Namely that you will die (in my

SILENCE

case). This can't be denied either. If you're on a plane and it crashes, your chances of dying are almost 100%. Only the chance of this happening is so incredibly small that you don't have to worry about it at all.

What helped me a lot is the following thoughts:

- I'm on a plane piloted by professionals who have been doing this for years;
- An airplane is proven to be safer than a ride in a car;
- Every aircraft is checked in advance;
- There are literally 30,000 planes flying in Europe every day and there have been very few accidents in the last 20 years;
- It's OK if the plane crashes if I don't survive;

But even though an airplane is safe, an airplane can still crash. You don't have 100% certainty. And you never will. Just like you can get a heart attack or crash your car.

Focus on how you feel, and let it be what is. The fact is, once you're on the plane nothing has happened yet. The only thing that makes you anxious is thinking about what might happen. Now anxiety about flying often does not start as soon as you are on the plane. For me, it often started a few days before I would get on the plane. And on the day itself, I was nervous all day because I knew I was about to board the plane.

It's also not the goal to never be anxious again when you get on a plane unless it controls your life. I still sometimes have catastrophic thoughts when I get on a plane. But I am "ok" with the sensations and thoughts that I have.

You can tackle the anxiety of heights in the same way as the anxiety of spiders. Debunk your catastrophic thoughts. Will you really die or will something serious happen if you get on the roller coaster or jump off the high diving board? Does the balcony on the tenth floor really break if you stand on it? Will you win the grand prize in the lottery? Probably not.

When I was still very afraid of heights, I even got sweaty hands when watching a video on youtube where someone was hanging from a crane without protection. While I was 100% safe behind my monitor. If I had to jump off a mountain while gaming I got the same feeling in my stomach as if I was sliding down a very high slide.

Start with small steps. Watch some videos of people doing something at great heights. If that has no effect on you, you can start practicing in real life. Go to a pool with a small and high diving board. Try to get off the small diving board first. If possible, try to jump harder and harder so that you jump higher and higher. Then try jumping off the high diving board.

The anxiety program will start running with all sorts of disaster scenarios. Probably even before you even get into the pool. It's therefore important to negate these catastrophic thoughts in advance. What's the worst that could happen?

The ultimate way to accept your anxiety about heights is to trick your brain into thinking that you are actually at a great height while standing with both feet on the ground. You can simulate this with VR (Virtual Reality). You get closed glasses on your head and go on a virtual roller coaster ride. This seems so real that you will react as if you are really on a roller coaster ride. This way you can easily challenge your anxiety about heights while standing safely on the ground.

Social anxiety

Social anxiety is my favorite. I've suffered a lot from this. I was mostly afraid of what other people would think of me. And that had to do with the fact that I had to blush (red face) in almost

SILENCE

every social situation. What worked well for me is technique two, making your anxiety worse.
Instead of trying to stop my face from turning red, I started thinking:

> "I want to turn red NOW! Bring it on!"

A variation on this is to make matters worse:

> "I want to get as red as possible NOW! Give me everything you've got!"

Further debunking your catastrophic thoughts also worked very well for me. The basis of social anxiety is what other people will think of you. Two things are very important here:

- You're never going to find out what anyone actually thinks about you;
- How you think other people think about you isn't true.

Suppose you see two people you know and are talking to each other. They look your way and suddenly start laughing. Then thoughts pass by:

- "Are they laughing at me now"?
- "Am I wearing weird clothes or something"?
- "They are probably talking about situation X from last week."
- "Why are they laughing at me"?
- Etc, etc.

A simple technique that gives you direct answers to these questions is to debunk these thoughts. Is it really true what you think? Can you be 100% certain that it's true? Even if you walk up to these people and ask why they are laughing, they could easily lie. In other words, you'll never find out exactly what other people think of you. People can lie and you can't read minds. So the answer to all the questions you have is always the same: you don't know. You've probably experienced that you keep thinking about something that happened for a few days or even weeks. And eventually, you have the courage to ask that person what is going on. Then you find out it wasn't about you at all. Or that the person in question has long forgotten the incident. While you were spending days or weeks worrying about the situation...

It doesn't matter what other people think of you. You are who you are. Thinking about what other people think of you doesn't solve anything either. In fact, if you have to constantly ask people if something was about you, they will think you're weird!

Anxiety about driving

Anxiety about driving is very common. The most important step is to debunk your catastrophic thoughts. What is the core of your anxiety? What exactly are you afraid of? Then the second question is, is that really true? Will a bridge really collapse if you just happen to drive over it? Are you going to cause an accident when you're in the car? You can start looking for evidence for your catastrophic thoughts. How many tunnels and bridges have collapsed in the past 20 years?

There are many variations of driving anxiety:

- Driving in the dark
- Driving in bad weather
- Driving over bridges
- Driving through tunnels
- Traffic lights
- Causing an accident
- Losing control
- Nowhere to go (stuck in your car)
- Panic attacks while driving
- Traffic jams

SILENCE

- Etc.

People sometimes take a detour of literally tens or hundreds of kilometers. Because they are afraid that X will happen if they follow a certain route. By disproving your catastrophic thoughts, you'll first look for evidence. Is it really true?

- Are you really going to cause an accident if you drive at night or if the weather is bad? Has that ever happened?
- Will a bridge really collapse if you drive over it?
- Are you really losing control? Have you ever really lost control completely?
- Can you really go nowhere if you are in a traffic jam or at a traffic light? Or can you just get out of the car?
- Etc.

Once you've researched this, you can test this in a safe place. Only this time you will apply a technique from this book. One of the techniques you could use is to challenge your thoughts. Instead of being afraid to cause an accident, you will now try to cause an accident. Of course not really causing an accident but in your mind. Say to yourself:

- "I want to cause an accident NOW!"
- "I want to lose control NOW"
- "I want a panic attack NOW"

You can combine this technique with accepting the outcome. Accept the outcome. You never have 100% certainty. It's therefore not the intention that you will never cause an accident again. But that you are "ok" with the fact that you could possibly have an accident. The only thing you can control is your own car. You didn't get your driver's license for no reason. So you can drive quite well. In addition, you can pay 100% attention while driving, but that does not mean that everyone pays attention. Someone else can also cause an accident.

Johan

Maybe it's too much to drive yourself right now. Then ask a friend or family member to drive the route for you. Sit next to the driver and observe what happens to you and what you think while driving. Write down all the thoughts and try to apply one of the techniques.

Agoraphobia

Agoraphobia is also pretty common. About 1% of all people will experience this at some point in their lives. With agoraphobia, you are afraid that something will happen if you leave your safe environment (for example, your house). This is often accompanied by panic attacks.

- Anxiety of fainting in public places;
- Afraid that something will happen in public areas;
- Afraid of being chased;
- Afraid of having a panic attack in public;
- Afraid of not getting help if something happens;
- Etc.

At a certain point, something happens that makes you no longer dare to go down the street. This could be anything. Even walking out your own door can be a huge task. It doesn't really matter what the cause is. What works well for agoraphobia is:

- Debunking your catastrophic thoughts
- Challenging your thoughts and sensations

Every anxiety always starts with "What if..." thoughts and a disaster scenario. What happens to you when you step out the door? What are you afraid of? What is your disaster scenario? You then check whether this disaster scenario is correct. Is this really true? Is this really going to happen? Has it ever happened?

SILENCE

A panicky feeling is common with agoraphobia. What you could try is to completely reverse everything you do. If you're afraid of having a panic attack, try consciously evoking one. By saying to yourself:

> "If I step out the front door, I immediately want to have a panic attack. And preferably the worst panic attack I've ever had!"

The anxiety that's in you wants to be heard. That tension in your body arises because you don't listen to your anxiety. Welcome your anxiety. Welcome your thoughts. Let it come. Just let it happen.

It's also "ok" for someone to chase you. What happens if someone is chasing you? If you are afraid that someone is going to rob you, then go out on the street and don't take anything with you. You can also tell yourself that today you hope someone will chase you.

Agoraphobia goes hand in hand with social anxiety and a strong urge to control the situation. A panic attack has nothing to do with a situation. A panic attack is controlled by your brain. In fact, you have complete control over a panic attack. A panic attack does not come when you want to have a panic attack. You have reversed the control mechanism by wanting to prevent and stop a panic attack. And that's exactly why you get a panic attack or feel extremely tense. The next time you go out, say to yourself:

> "Just give me a panic attack. Then people just look at me. I don't care if someone chases me. It's OK".

By being "ok" with the outcome of the disaster scenario, anxiety has much less grip. Just let your disaster scenario happen. You can also practice it at home first. By standing in front of a mirror

Johan

and evoking the tense feeling that you normally experience outside.

Another technique you can use is making your anxiety absurd with humor. Before you go out, come up with an extreme disaster scenario. Make it a complete comedy show. That you are chased, thrown in a van, and that you wake up on a deserted island. Then a big yacht passes by with your favorite actor. Then you have conversations about your personal lives etc. Maybe you can get a role in his or her next big movie!

Chapter 28: Conclusion and Closing

Anxiety and panic follow a pattern. This pattern is always the same. I like to call this the anxiety program. This program is programmed in everybody's mind, no exception. You can do many things with this program but there is one thing you can't do: delete it or try to stop it. When you are trying to get rid of your anxiety, you are trying to delete the anxiety program. The solution is stop trying to get rid of your anxiety and start greeting. Whatever you do, always keep this in mind.

I want to close this book with an exercise.

Exercise: the anxiety filter

1. Sit on a chair or couch;
2. Put your hands out in front of you and spread your fingers;
3. Bring your left hand in front of your face so that you are looking at the world through your fingers;
4. Then bring your right hand in front of your face and place it over your left hand;
5. If all goes well, you now have two hands in front of your eyes, both with fingers spread. Looking at the space where you are currently sitting is difficult but you can still see somewhat through the gaps of your fingers;
6. Take one or two minutes and look through your fingers at the space where you are currently sitting;
7. After two minutes, remove your hands and place both with open palms on your legs.

Your hands and fingers are your anxiety. They cloud your vision and you no longer see clearly what is actually happening in the world. Now try to get rid of your hands by thinking…

Johan

Can you make your hands disappear by thinking about it? Sure, you can lower your hands so they don't block your vision but can you really make them disappear? No you can't! Each time you want to get rid of some emotional problem, think about this exercise. You can never make it go away by thinking about or wishing it away. And it doesn't have to go away! Just like you can lower your hands so they don't block your vision anymore. You can also stop the anxiety program from running. You just need to stop trying to change or get rid of it. **It can stay!**

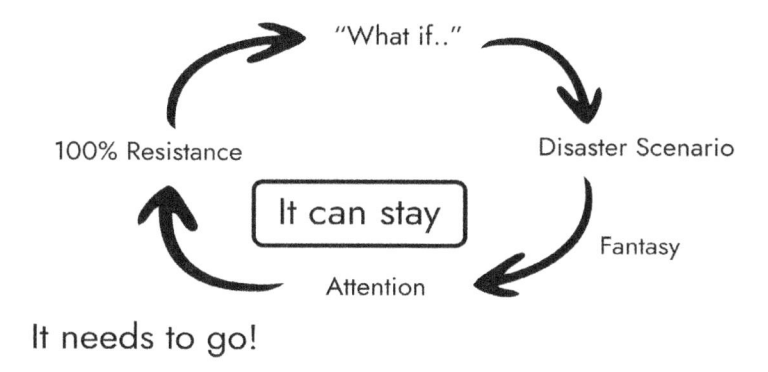

```
                    "What if.."
        
   100% Resistance           Disaster Scenario
        
              ┌─────────────┐
              │ It can stay │
              └─────────────┘
                                Fantasy
                  Attention
```

It needs to go!

This is the end of my book. I've tried to give as many different examples of anxiety and associated techniques as possible. Although I experienced many anxieties and panic attacks, it may well be that you have other things at play that are not covered in this book. You can ask me questions about your specific anxiety (info@anxietyisok.com) or if things in the book aren't clear.

And very important: **keep practicing!**

You must take action. Make a plan. Which exercises do you want to start with? Take your time. Don't jump to the next book or therapy when you're done reading this book. Take action. Research what works well for you in practice. You can do it!

SILENCE

Good luck!

Johan

Johan

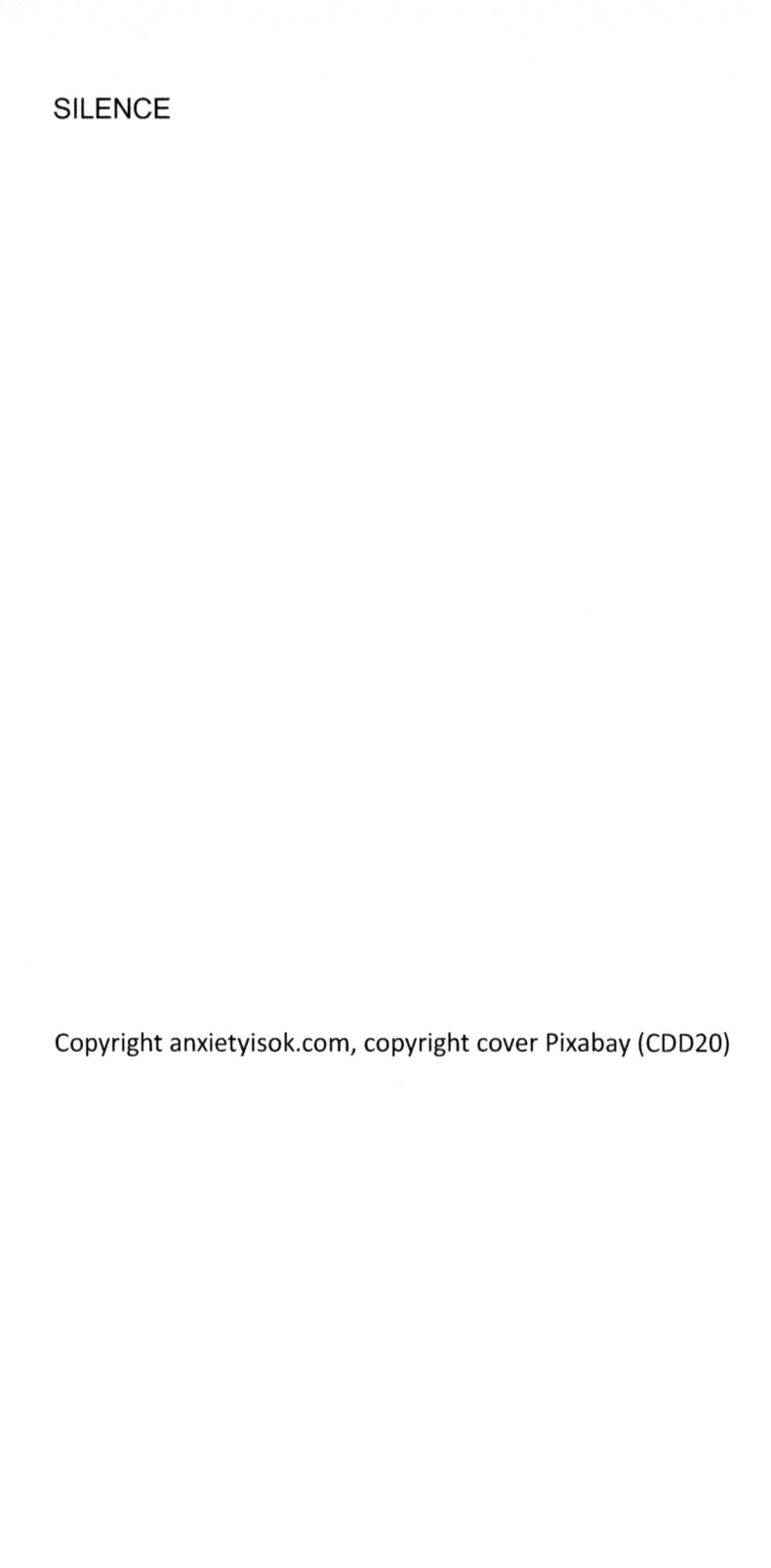

SILENCE

Copyright anxietyisok.com, copyright cover Pixabay (CDD20)

Printed in Great Britain
by Amazon